Leaves from a prison diary, or, Lectures to a "solitary" audience. Volume 1 of 2

Michael Davitt

The Making of Modern Law collection of legal archives constitutes a genuine revolution in historical legal research because it opens up a wealth of rare and previously inaccessible sources in legal, constitutional, administrative, political, cultural, intellectual, and social history. This unique collection consists of three extensive archives that provide insight into more than 300 years of American and British history. These collections include:

Legal Treatises, 1800-1926: over 20,000 legal treatises provide a comprehensive collection in legal history, business and economics, politics and government.

Trials, 1600-1926: nearly 10,000 titles reveal the drama of famous, infamous, and obscure courtroom cases in America and the British Empire across three centuries.

Primary Sources, 1620-1926: includes reports, statutes and regulations in American history, including early state codes, municipal ordinances, constitutional conventions and compilations, and law dictionaries.

These archives provide a unique research tool for tracking the development of our modern legal system and how it has affected our culture, government, business – nearly every aspect of our everyday life. For the first time, these high-quality digital scans of original works are available via print-on-demand, making them readily accessible to libraries, students, independent scholars, and readers of all ages.

The BiblioLife Network

This project was made possible in part by the BiblioLife Network (BLN), a project aimed at addressing some of the huge challenges facing book preservationists around the world. The BLN includes libraries, library networks, archives, subject matter experts, online communities and library service providers. We believe every book ever published should be available as a high-quality print reproduction; printed on-demand anywhere in the world. This insures the ongoing accessibility of the content and helps generate sustainable revenue for the libraries and organizations that work to preserve these important materials.

The following book is in the "public domain" and represents an authentic reproduction of the text as printed by the original publisher. While we have attempted to accurately maintain the integrity of the original work, there are sometimes problems with the original work or the micro-film from which the books were digitized. This can result in minor errors in reproduction. Possible imperfections include missing and blurred pages, poor pictures, markings and other reproduction issues beyond our control. Because this work is culturally important, we have made it available as part of our commitment to protecting, preserving, and promoting the world's literature.

GUIDE TO FOLD-OUTS MAPS and OVERSIZED IMAGES

The book you are reading was digitized from microfilm captured over the past thirty to forty years. Years after the creation of the original microfilm, the book was converted to digital files and made available in an online database.

In an online database, page images do not need to conform to the size restrictions found in a printed book. When converting these images back into a printed bound book, the page sizes are standardized in ways that maintain the detail of the original. For large images, such as fold-out maps, the original page image is split into two or more pages

Guidelines used to determine how to split the page image follows:

• Some images are split vertically; large images require vertical and horizontal splits.
• For horizontal splits, the content is split left to right.
• For vertical splits, the content is split from top to bottom.
• For both vertical and horizontal splits, the image is processed from top left to bottom right.

LEAVES FROM A PRISON DIARY;

OR,

LECTURES TO A "SOLITARY" AUDIENCE.

The Prison Cell

LEAVES

FROM

A PRISON DIARY;

Or, Lectures to a "Solitary" Audience.

BY

MICHAEL DAVITT

FOUNDER OF THE LAND LEAGUE

IN TWO VOLUMES

VOLUME I

LONDON CHAPMAN AND HALL,

LIMITED.

1885.

LONDO

L. CLAY, SONS, AND TAYL

BREAD STREET HILL

DEC ～ 191

Dedication.

TO THE

MEMORY OF THE LITTLE CONFIDING FRIEND

WHOSE PLAYFUL MOODS

AND LOVING FAMILIARITY

HELPED TO CHEER THE SOLITUDE OF A CONVICT CELL;

TO MY

PET BLACKBIRD, "JOE,"

THESE PRISON JOTTINGS

ARE AFFECTIONATELY DEDICATED.

PREFACE.

I was remitted to Portland Prison on the 3rd of February, 1881 Shortly afterwards, through the kindness of the governor, a young blackbird came into my possession. For some months I relieved the tedium of my solitude by efforts to win the confidence of my companion, with the happiest results. He would stand upon my breast as I lay in bed in the morning and awaken me from sleep. He would perch upon the edge of my plate and share my porridge. His familiarity was such that on showing him a small piece of slate pencil, and then placing it in my waistcoat pocket, he would immediately abstract it. He would perch upon the edge of my slate as it was adjusted between my knees, and watching the course of the pencil as I wrote, would make the most amusing efforts to peck the marks from off the slate. He would "fetch and carry" as faithfully as any well-trained dog. Towards evening he would resort to his perch, the post of the iron bedstead, and there remain, silent and still, till the dawning of another day, when his chirrup would again be heard, like the voice of Nature, before the herald of civilisation, the clang of the prison bell at five o'clock.

One evening as "Joe" sat upon his perch, it occurred to me to constitute him chairman and audience of a course of lectures, and with him constantly before me as the representative of my fellow creatures, I jotted down what I have substantially reproduced in the following pages.

CONTENTS.

LECTURE VIII.

BOGUS NOBLEMEN,

LECTURE IX

BOGUS NOBLEMEN (*continued*).

LECTURE X.

CLASS III   MAGSMEN (*continued*).

LECTURE XI.

CLASS III. SECTION 2 "HOOKS"

LECTURE XII

CLASS III. "HOOKS" (continued).

LECTURE XIII.

CLASS IV.

LECTURE XIV.

LECTURE XV

LECTURE XVI.

CRIMINAL VANITY.

LECTURE XVII

PRISON "POETS'

CONTENTS.

PART II.

SOCIAL EVILS AND SUGGESTED REMEDIES.

LECTURE XXI.

THE PUNISHMENT OF PENAL SERVITUDE.

LEAVES FROM A PRISON DIARY

OR,

Lectures to a "Solitary" Audience.

INTRODUCTION.

MR CHAIRMAN,—Three months have now elapsed since the day upon which you rashly ventured from the paternal nest, and nearly fell a victim to the Infirmary grimalkin. Although you would, naturally enough, prefer the guardianship of your parents to that under which you have been placed as a consequence of your youthful temerity, your trust in the ministering care of a being whom instinct teaches you to dread as an enemy shows that you appreciate my efforts to make you as happy as imprisonment will allow. I know, however, that when you are a few months older and strong enough to provide for yourself, your desire to be free will no longer find me capable of resisting your right to liberty.

You shall be free; though your liberation will leave me once more to the fellowship of whitewashed walls and a dreary solitude.

I shall miss your chirrup greeting of a morning, as well as your company at our frugal breakfast. You will no more "run and fetch" the pellets of paper to place upon my knee and await the signal for another chase along our cell floor.

Other cares and delights will occupy you then Your favourite perch—the post of the cell bedstead—after the day's routine of romp and recreation is over, will know you no more. In its place you will have the waving bough and leafy shade of some tall sycamore, from whence you will serenade your more congenial mate, and view the beauties of some smiling landscape. Happy in your natural sphere, you will join in the general concert of Nature in vocal praise of the bounteous Author of the bright and joyous external world.

Pending this hour of separation, you shall be both "chairman and audience" of a course of lectures Our evenings will suffice for this work; and, as an inducement to obtain from you an attentive and patient hearing, I promise most faithfully that you shall be restored to liberty the day after the delivery of the last lecture of the series

Not knowing what impressions you may have formed

of the strange beings whom you see moving about the
prison grounds every day, I shall devote our first
lectures to the task of enlightening you upon the
matter—their crimes, and how they perform them;
their schemes and dodges, their opinions on men and
things deemed to be moral; their general habits and
characteristics; exploits in criminal pursuits; slang
and literature, their religion, &c I shall next speak
of the causes which act as recruiting agencies for so
many huge criminal institutions like that in which
we now are, and conclude by pointing out such remedies
for the diminution of ignorance, poverty, pauperism,
and crime as seem to me to be both just and feasible,
and which, if only carried out in time by wise states-
manship, would minimise that social injustice which
begets the sense of wrong and discontent in the minds
of the labouring masses, and the consequent desire for
revolutionary change that are now disturbing society,
and preparing the way for a great social upheaval in
nearly every civilised country.

In dealing with the various types of criminal represented in this prison, I will follow the prison rule and
classify them by their conduct instead of by their crimes
or sentences, and I will then analyse each class and describe the various criminal pursuits represented therein.
It is only by a knowledge of their acts and schemes of
crime when at war with society, and by an insight into

their behaviour when under disciplinary restraint, that the problems of their proper punishment and moral reclamation can best be studied Still, I must not be understood as agreeing that such classification is the best that could be adopted for a convict establishment. My knowledge of each class of criminal to be found in these prisons convinces me that the most irreclaimable thief is often the best conducted individual in the place ; and from this seeming inconsistency between an ingrained criminal disposition on the one hand, and an apparent excellence of behaviour while undergoing the rigours of penal discipline on the other, I draw the argument in favour of a classification that would remove such men from really well-conducted prisoners less hardened in crime.

In one of our later discourses I shall deal more fully with the subject of proper prison classification.

To describe the ordinary criminal so that he may be seen in every phase of his immoral individuality, will necessitate the giving of such particulars of his schemes of crime as some may possibly object to, on the grounds of a too close examination of an undesirable subject. But in the interests of that society against which he wars, as well as for the ultimate good of the criminal himself, it appears to me to be necessary to expose such of the general thieving *modus operandi* as I have learned from my forced association with professional criminals;

and I am persuaded that this can be done without in any way encouraging crime or trenching in the least upon a due regard for the ordinary decencies of expression. Many crimes are committed as much through the prevalence of a careless handling and a needless display of wealth by the moneyed class, as through the stealing propensities of the thief. The astounding "simplicity" of other classes in society affords yet another field for the operations of criminal minds. The victims of long firms, bogus banks, insurance swindles, confidence-trick workers, begging-letter writers, card sharpers, and the rest of the "magsmen" fraternity, are mostly themselves responsible for the crime thus perpetrated; and an *exposé* of how they allow themselves to be deluded by these subterfuges may possibly reduce the number of offences under such heads in future.

Again, there is a class of crime upon which I intend to touch that is seldom brought to light in the police courts, owing to the stigma which, upon its discovery, attaches to those who allow themselves to become its victims. It is most prevalent in London and other large cities, and trading upon it becomes the *rôle* which those superannuated jail-birds play who know how willing any man who falls into their traps would be to allow himself to be blackmailed rather than become ruined in character by the publicity which a prosecution would entail   Hence a lucrative but infamous game is played with almost perfect impunity by thieves who are no longer able to carry on the schemes of their earlier criminal days.

We may possibly be able to render some little service to the public, and perhaps to the morals of society as well, while we are shut up here, by a few lectures on these phases of criminal life, which can see the light of the outer world by and by; while our exposition of the plans and dodges of professional theft may save many a poor wretch not yet fallen from the frightful penalty of penal servitude

But all our evening talks shall not be upon men and things exclusively criminal.   We will reveal, in some of our discourses, whatever little silver lining there is to be found behind the dark cloud of imprisonment. True, this will be but a negative description of penal consolation.   All is not despair and heartache within stone walls, even with daily tasks of forced labour, and a consciousness of years of loss of liberty added.   Among so many thousands of unfortunates, all humanity is not of a repulsive nature, and it will be a pleasure to dwell upon such traits of character as have fallen under my observation which show that all is not lost to moral sense and honour beneath the ban of penal servitude

Thus progressing from bad to better we shall come to the wider and more congenial field of society beyond these walls, and inquire into those of its conditions of social organisation which begot not only the larger part of the crime we shall have to dwell upon by and by, but the mass of wretchedness and poverty that presses upon the lives of millions who work, but who have to surrender too much of their earnings and their liberties to those who neither toil nor spin. We shall conclude, as I have already indicated, with an endeavour to point out how those blessings of liberty and peace, so long and ardently yearned for by true reformers, but "still imprisoned in an imperfect freedom," may be evolved from existing political and social systems, and brought within the reach and enjoyment of all.

PART I.

CRIMINAL LIFE AND CHARACTER.

LECTURE I.

Introductory—A Burglar's Definition of Natural Law—Robbing a Thief—Criminal Physiognomy—Murder in its relation to other Crimes—Conduct of Murderers in Penal Servitude—Classification of Criminals in a Convict Prison—Flogging a Lawyer—Crime represented in Class I

POPE has said—

> 'Vice is a monster of so frightful mien
> As, to be hated, needs but to be seen ;
> Yet seen too oft, familiar with her face,
> We first endure, then pity, then embrace."

If for the last two words in these oft-quoted lines the poet had been able to substitute "then wish to efface," he would have rendered an accurate description of the feelings which contact with the criminal classes evoke in the minds of those who may be compelled to associate with them. If the amount of human vice which Clerkenwell, Newgate, Millbank, Dartmoor, Portsmouth, and Portland prisons (prisons over which my experience extends), shut in for a time from mingling

with what is undetected in the external world, could
have formed a picture in the mind of the author of the
above lines, he would have shuddered a great deal more
at its contemplation, and satirist of mankind though he
was, he would scarcely have enumerated as one of its
weaknesses the possibility of embracing a monster so
truly hideous.

Pity, however, is the predominant feeling which so
much moral deformity excites in the breast of an
ordinary mortal who is doomed to behold the ruin
which it has made of so many fellow-creatures—pity
not unmixed with some indignation at the causes
that are mainly responsible for the careers of such ab-
normal beings   But what of the society against which
these modern Ishmaelites have turned their hands
and schemes of crime? Is it not, in some measure,
deserving alike of the attacks to which it is subjected
by such a large and dangerous class, and to this reproach upon its vaunted civilisation, for the criminal
negligence it has shown towards the waifs and strays
of city and town—the children of criminals and of
pauperism, whose training in theft and dishonesty has
been going on beneath its very eyes until a regular
criminal class of hardened and educated thieves and
vagabonds demands the existence of an enormous and
expensive system of police detection?

One of these educated thieves one day observed to

me—"The laws of society are framed for the purpose of securing the wealth of the world to power and calculation, thereby depriving the larger portion of mankind of its rights and chances. Why should they punish me for taking by somewhat similar means from those who have taken more than they had a right to? My dear sir," said he, "I deny your contention that there is any such thing as honesty in the world at all." This belief is common to all the types of criminal pursuit. The poverty and squalor in which the children of the poor are reared, the next to total neglect of their moral training at the age when ideas of right and wrong ought to be inculcated by means of precept and example, and the crowning influence of drunken, depraved, or indifferent parents, are the sources from which such education is derived, and out of which two-thirds of the criminal life of these countries has sprung.

The individual to whom I have already alluded was a fellow-worker of mine for nigh two years in Dartmoor. He had, in his younger days, passed through the workhouse; read the pestilent literature of rascaldom which has educated so many criminal characters in this country; then graduated in the "School" (as the existing reformatories are familiarly termed by thieves), and ultimately became a noted burglar His reading in prison had been pretty extensive, while his intelligence

would have insured him a position in society above
that of a labouring man, if it had had a substratum of
moral principle to rest upon, instead of the teaching of
vicious surroundings and examples which had poisoned
his youthful mind. I could not help looking upon it
as a very novel experience, for even this grotesque
world, to have to listen to a man who could delight in
a literary discussion, quote all the choice parts of Pope's
Iliad, and boast of having read Pascal and Lafontaine
in the original, maintain, in sober argument, that
"thieving was an *honourable* pursuit," and that religion,
law, patriotism, and bodily disease were the real and
only enemies of humanity. "Religion," he would
observe, "robbed the soul of its independence, while
society's social laws, in restraining the desires and
faculties given by Nature to man for the purpose of
gratification, declared war against the manifest spirit
of the law of our being." Patriotism he termed " the
idolatry of an idea, in the stupid worship of which the
peace of the world, and well-being of its inhabitants,
were sacrificed by the law-makers and others who profit
thereby." And so on with all other principles and
customs that indicate men or society to be progressing
towards a higher degree of moral or religious perfection.
All men were, according to his conception of man's use
of life, but superior animals, and all who warred against
the laws which denied to man the gratification of his

natural appetites were engaged in an "honourable" pursuit.

I one day missed my labour "chum" from his place in our "push" or gang, and learned that he had "nosed" another prisoner, that is, struck him a blow on that organ, and was undergoing three days' "chokey" (bread and water) for indulging in such a luxury I asked him, on his release, what he had done it for, and learned that it was because another prisoner had gone into his cell during his absence and stolen his bread. "But is not thieving an honourable pursuit?" I ventured to object. "Well, yes," he replied; "but I punched him not so much for stealing my bread as for sneaking into my cell like a 'cadger' when I was not there. We people look upon a theft from one of ourselves as you do upon such an act being perpetrated in a church—it is sacrilege against the order"

Human passion and impulse having little or no scope for exercise within the rigid limits of prison discipline, the observation of these disturbing elements of society, when in a state of compression or inactivity, is as interesting to the student of humanity as it is occasionally fruitful of eccentric and mirth-provoking occurrences. The common notion, so prevalent among the novel-reading and other portions of the public, that the criminal classes, or *habitués* of prisons, are all of a Bill Sykes, or similar physiognomic stamp of character, is as untrue and misleading as would be the supposition that all people who go to church must be saints, or, at least, holy people. The cleverest burglars I have ever conversed with, as well as the most noted swindlers with whom I have been in forced association, might pass in society for members of quite opposite professions. The man-brute whom Dickens has portrayed, and whom the comic journals reproduce in their cartoons as the type of the most dangerous criminal order, is not as frequently met with in a convict prison as is generally believed. The closest approach to him in convict society is the cowardly bully who is known by the term "bruiser" in prison slang, and who is usually the hanger-on of some unfortunate creature who supports him out of the rewards of her shame. I have conversed in prison with over twenty, and have been for years a close observer of several other murderers, without being able to trace a predilection to that greatest of all crimes, either in the conduct or facial expressions of these individuals. Murder might really be what De Quincey has termed one of the fine arts for anything an observer of this portion of prison popula-tion could discern in the ordinary shaped heads, general observance of prison discipline, and personal behaviour of most murderers. The really hardened, irreclaimable criminal will never commit a murder. Neither will that nearest approach to Bill Sykes in style of dress and face, the bruiser. Robbery with violence these will commit, thrash a policeman, or give cruel ill-treatment to the wretched beings with whom they cohabit, but they have too wholesome a dread of being "topped" (hanged) to add murder to their list of other accomplishments. Murders occasionally occur in connection with robbery, it is true, but they are as a rule accidental to the perpetration of the latter crime, and scarcely ever premeditated. The most heinous of all offences— murder deliberately intended and planned before its commission—is, ordinarily, the offspring of the passions of revenge and jealousy, or the outcome of social or political wrongs, and is more frequently the result of some derangement of the nobler instincts of human nature than traceable to its more debased orders or appetites. Temporary insanity, parental mania (as when mothers or fathers murder their whole family), and infanticide, add their quota to this class of crime; but it stands in no relationship, in its ultimate motives, to the other numerous crimes which bring together in a convict establishment such a variety of criminal character.

Taking a convict prison of, say, twelve hundred men (which will be about the average roll of the convict establishments in England), it will be found that six hundred of these pass through their terms of imprisonment with exemplary conduct, that is, without a single report having been made against them for breach of discipline—a discipline probably without a parallel in its treatment of human temper in any other services, civil or military, in the world.

Three hundred more will be reckoned well-conducted prisoners by the governor, having occasional reports, but none of serious or insubordinate description. Two hundred and fifty more will comprise very troublesome prisoners, that is, men of a refractory disposition and guilty of occasional outbursts, against whom there are frequent reports; while the remaining fifty will be almost entirely unmanageable, desperate in their attacks upon fellow-prisoners, and occasionally upon prison warders, and apparently insensible alike to the kind advice of chaplain or priest, or of any leniency or punishment at the hands of sterner officials. It is by prisoners of the latter class that warders have been occasionally murdered in convict prisons.

Compulsory association with these four classes, into which the whole criminal prison population of England and Scotland may be divided, enables me, after nine years of contact and frequent conversation with hundreds of each class, to form the following observations upon their criminal dispositions or character, and to give the subsequent illustrations of their plans of operation when out of prison.

CLASS I.—A section of this class will never have been in prison before, and will have had no contact, previous to imprisonment, with what is known to the police as "the criminal classes." Forgers, bigamists, men convicted for indecent assaults, men who have been found guilty of systematic fraudulent practices in connection with business or professional pursuits, will belong to this class in prison. Lawyers are occasionally met with in convict dress, and it is but fair to the love of law peculiar to the limbs thereof to state that the prison conduct of the few members of the profession who are detected in crime and convicted is such as ranks them with the best conducted prisoners. There was but one exception to this rule in my experience of this class of convict. He, on one occasion, forgot the use of his tongue in an argument with a warder, and fell back upon "the logic of a blow." Verdict by the visiting director, "two dozen lashes with the cat"—a sentence which, doubtless, impressed the said lawyer's back very much with the force of new and unanswerable reasoning.

By far the greater portion of the six hundred prisoners, however, comprised within Class I. will be made up of old jail-birds—men who are thoroughly inured to crime, but who are too familiar with the penalties of insubordination, from former prison experience, to invite extra punishment by coming into

conflict with the rules and regulations. All the
schemes of theft and swindling that are to be described in future lectures will have professors among
this, exceptionally well-behaved section of a prison
population

The remaining portion of Class I. will comprise
receivers of stolen goods, or "buyers"—men who will
have had contact with burglars and other criminals
outside—horse and cattle thieves, men convicted for
manslaughter, and murderers. Religious, or "parsons'
and priests'" men, as they are designated by ungodly
prisoners, are mostly confined to this class, the singular
feature of which is this, that although it represents
almost every species of crime found in the calendar,
and is the one of the four classes from which society
has suffered most depredations, the conduct of its
members while undergoing penal servitude will
more than favourably compare with the highest
examples of patience and fortitude known to the
student of frail humanity.

LECTURE II.

CLASS II.   THE THIEVOCRACY.

"Honourable" Thieves—Criminal Ambition—A Sham Hero
Burglar—Yarn of "Flash Johnson"—Accomplishments of
Burglars—Market Price of Booty—Women Accomplices—
Their Plans of Theft—Self-sacrifice.

CLASS II.—To this class belongs both the higher and
middle ranks of the aristocracy of crime—professional
burglars, "honourable" thieves, professional swindlers,
members of the "long firm," and dealers in "snide"
(base coin)   Ninety per cent of this class will
have more or less acquaintance with minor imprisonment before entering penal servitude, while
many "professors" will reckon from two to four experiences of convict life   This class looks with contempt upon all "low" thieves, and repudiates the
mean or "cadger" order of crime as discreditable to
the profession of thieving. They form the most singular
and interesting study of all the criminal classes. It is

to them that the phrase "honour among thieves" refers. They never "round" upon each other, while they hold all "coppers" (prison informers) in detestation. They are an intelligent class of men, as a rule, though very deficient in common sense and common prudence in the regulation of their ordinary conduct when out of prison. Regard for honesty, religion, or morality they have none whatever, except what portion of the latter virtue may be comprised within the practice not to rob or betray an associate, or operate upon the working or poorer classes when prosecuting their "honourable" calling in society Had their earlier years been identified with other than criminal associations, they would belong to the skilled artisan class of Englishmen. All the mechanical work required in a convict prison is performed by their labour.

To be considered a member of this order, and be credited with having done a "big job" in one's time, is the ambition of the less accomplished thieves, and is what they invariably report themselves to be among "flats," i.e the ignorant section of convicts who are outside the "profession" London, of course, supplies the greater portion of this class to the convict prisons, and these metropolitan adepts in crime have a very inferior opinion of all the provincial or foreign artists belonging to the same calling. Numbers of them have travelled abroad, and have tried their hands and tools

in Belgium, France, and America. They all agree in
the opinion that the latter is the most difficult and
dangerous country in which to do a "burst" (burglary).
The Yankees are admitted to be very 'cute in guarding
their wealth, and make very little scruple in giving the
contents of a revolver to any one who ventures for those
of a desk or safe   I have conversed with several
cracksmen who have been in Egypt, Russia, Turkey,
and other foreign lands. Many of them while in prison
study French, German, mechanics, and chemistry; and
I have found a good few clever linguists among their
number   In reply to questions as to why they did not
turn their energies and talents to honest and industrial
pursuits, their answer, as a general rule, was that there
is an amount of excitement and pleasure in the life of
a cracksman unknown in that of an ordinary wage-paid
toiler   Efforts to reform this class rarely if ever prove
successful   Their good conduct in prison is partly the
outcome of a resolve not to bring additional punishment upon themselves, or to prolong their imprisonment
by insubordination, and partly the result of experience
produced by former terms of imprisonment   They are
generally sold or betrayed to the detectives by the
abandoned creatures with whom they spend the "swag"
after a successful enterprise. They declare this to be the
way in which they are "lagged" (arrested), when not
taken in the performance of a "job," and not through

the cleverness of the detectives   They consequently
hold the fair sex in far less estimation, as human beings,
than either Turk or Heathen Chinee

When a young thief belonging to the next class
wishes to pass himself off on a "flat" as a professional, he will ask his auditor if he knows Nobby
from the Dials, Jack Somebody from the New Cut,
or Bill Somethingelse from Golden Lane ; adding super-
lative slang encomiums to the particular forte of each,
and recounting with an I-took-part-myself-in-it air such
recent burglaries or clever "lifts" as may have excited
unusual interest in the public press

I well recollect the excitement which the advent
of one of these sham heroes to the exercise yard of
Millbank caused among the pick-pocket fraternity,
after he had announced himself as having got seven
"stretch" (years) for clearing out a jeweller's shop in
Manchester. He had "planted the swag" (hid the
plunder) before being caught, where it would be safe
until he was "chucked up" (released), when he would
dispose of it in Belgium or Holland, buy a racehorse,
and live the life of a swell in future.   Lord Wolseley
recounting his exploits amid a company of volunteers
or new recruits would not excite half the envy which
this young thief, who was known as "Flash Johnson,"
created in the convict circle into which his sentence
introduced him.   He preceded me to Dartmoor, where

I found his fame even more loudly trumpeted than ever, especially by Manchester "hooks" (pick-pockets), who boast of being the rivals of the "Cocks," or Londoners, in the art of obtaining other people's property without paying for it. Unfortunately for fame that does not rest upon actual deeds, and for reputation not genuinely acquired, one of Flash Johnson's "pals" arrived in Dartmoor one day, in company with a fresh batch of prisoners from Millbank, and soon brought down the renown of the hitherto worshipped hero to the very dust, by relating that there was not a word of truth in Johnson's yarn; as he had been "lagged" for having "sneaked" a costermonger's barrow and contents! Johnson never lifted his diminished head again during his stay in Dartmoor; and doubtless his ambition upon regaining liberty will be to perform some "great act" which will entitle him to the envy and admiration of his companions in crime.

Not the least efficacious of the remedies proposed for the diminishing of the criminal classes would be the entire separation of the young pick-pockets of first convictions from the criminals I am treating of in this sketch of Class II. while in prison

I found many of this class to be men of very good address, possessing a fair knowledge of political and passing events, and bearing little or no trace of their following in any of their belongings, except in their use of slang expressions. They would pass in hotels or in railway trains as men of business among people who would have no experience of criminal character. They may be divided into experts or scientific, and less skilled, thieves The former make hotels, jewellers'-shops, offices, and mansions where valuable plate is known to be, their field of operation; not despising lower booty should a good chance present itself of obtaining it. They will often spend weeks, and sometimes months, in maturing their plans for a big "burst," and work in partnerships of two or more, as the nature of the "job" may require To obtain the requisite knowledge of the interior of a place which is "spotted" for operations, the game of "sweethearting the slavey" is gone through by the best-looking member of the gang If a certain number of interviews with a servant can thus be obtained, it becomes an easy matter to learn the habits of the household, the character for vigilance of the nearest "bobby," and the other necessary particulars for the successful carrying out of the "burst"

Burglars seldom receive more than twenty per cent of the value of their booty from the buyers to whom they dispose of it, if it happens to be in any other form than coin A 10*l* Bank of England note will bring but 2*l*. from a buyer, while 100*l*. worth of plate would be only worth 15*l* or 20*l* to the thief who would risk years of liberty in obtaining it, and so on of all other valuables If the stories told by these criminals can be credited, many men of apparent stainless character in the commercial world owe most of their wealth to direct dealing with professional thieves

The less skilled section of this class work in a peculiar manner, generally having a woman as an accomplice The "lady' is often the direct agent in obtaining the "swag" She is not a prostitute, but cohabits with her partner as long as they are mutually agreeable, and profitable, to each other. The possession of one of these lady artists who may be renowned for cleverness, is an object of much desire and professional wooing among her male admirers Two essential points in her equipment must be good looks and ladylike address and carriage, as these are the weapons with which she operates She must, above all things, be well dressed.

Thus "rigged," she makes her descent upon a fashionable jeweller, or dealer in other costly articles of female luxury, often driving to the establishment in a respectable hired carriage. Her plan is to obtain the inspection of as many valuable articles as possible before making a purchase, exhibiting a make-believe well-filled purse, &c , while engaged in examining the goods, then buying a few trifles, and pilfering whatever can be secured without the knowledge of the dealer or shopman. All the arts known to the class of mortals termed "coquettes" may be called into requisition for exercise in an enterprise of this description; while "palming" diamonds, exchanging paste for genuine jewellery, &c., form additional parts of the lady's accomplishments   The "gentleman" is usually on guard outside, ready to secure the "swag" when "Miss Courtney, of Belgravia," or "Miss Florence Beaumont, of Kensington," shall have completed her purchases and be driven away

When the male professor tries his hand in his particular line, the lady becomes the aide-de-camp   A Miss Brown, Jones, or Robinson. from London, Manchester, or Glasgow, puts up at some first-class country hotel, watering-place, or other such resort of fashionable people, where numerous guests are known to be staying. A Mr. Wilberforce, or some other respectably sounding name, will arrive a day before or after, at the same hotel, from some city or place in the country, and stay a week or two. No intercourse will take place between the accomplices while in the hotel, at least to the observation of the other guests   The gentleman, after becoming acquainted with the house, and discovering where the parties are located who are believed to have most cash or valuables, will go to work in day or night, as best suits his plans; and with skeleton-keys help himself to whatever plunder may fall in his way. This is usually given to Miss Brown for security, who will be one of the first to report the loss of her purse, or gold watch, after the thief has absconded. As a rule, the proprietors prefer making good the damage rather than allow their hotels to figure in the papers as having harboured such characters, and thereby sustain discredit to its reputation as a safe and respectable house. Miss Brown, Jones, or Robinson leaves, of course, in a few days afterwards, loudly complaining, and resolving never to stay in another hotel without giving her jewels or valuables to the proprietor on her arrival.

The lady thief also lends assistance when a burglary is to be attempted in a street or open thoroughfare, where the "copper" patrols. To do this requires that she shall play the part of an unfortunate, to the extent of parading in the neighbourhood, while she is acting as a sentinel on the policeman, during the time that her chums are making an entrance in, or clearing out, the place selected for the "burst." Should the policeman make his appearance at a critical point of the operation, the woman will feign drunkenness, "go for" the policeman's whisker, and allow herself to be taken into custody, screaming, struggling, and employing other feminine stratagems while in the act of being "run in." She may get seven, fourteen, or twenty-one days in the Bridewell for creating a disturbance in the public streets, but her confederates will, in all probability, have succeeded in their little game, through her self-sacrificing action having removed the enemy from the immediate neighbourhood of the enterprise

LECTURE III.

Professional Swindlers—Long Firm Workers—Exploits of an
Accomplished Rogue—He Runs a Long Firm—Cheating a
Home Secretary in the Home Office—Using the Name of
His Grace of Argyll—How to Advertise a Quack Nostrum

THE two sections of Class II., thus briefly sketched,
may be considered "the criminal upper ten" They
are held in the highest estimation by their humbler
brethren, who envy the possession of such talents and
good fortune as have enabled so many of them to write
their names in daring or historic "bursts" in the
London weekly press records of burglary fame They
never pick pockets, as they hold such low occupation as
far beneath the status of an "honourable thief," as
would a duke or a marquis the task of wheeling a
barrow They are generally worn out by the combined
effects of imprisonment, intemperance, and disease
before they reach fifty years of age

The remaining section of this class—professional
swindlers, members of the "long firm," and utterers

of base coin, or "snide pitchers"—may also be ranked as "honourable,' inasmuch as they profess only to victimise "those who can afford it, you know" They refuse to sell a comrade or pick a pocket Like their aristocratic brethren of the "jemmy and file," they will mostly all have put in various terms of previous imprisonments, made up of short sentences in county bridewells; some, of course, counting one or more "laggings,' or acquaintances with penal servitude, in addition As a rule, they are better educated than the members of the preceding class, the "snide pitchers" excepted. Ignorance would never enable them to prosecute their special callings with much chance of success

Excepting the "snide pitchers," it would be very difficult to describe the various ways in which these men play upon society. They do not confine themselves to any particular plan in the pursuit of their various professions, and may be said, truly, to live by their wits—like the "magsmen" and begging-letter writers who belong to the next class Bogus insurance companies and banks; contribution cards and sheets for obtaining subscriptions towards "charitable or religious purposes;" sham prospectuses in connection with reputed commercial or business enterprises, &c, are among the number of dodges to which they resort for the attainment of plunder. They are the class by which "long firms" are run, and, as is well known, by aid of which confiding individuals or innocent traders are so often "sold," when believing themselves only selling. This 'long firm" work is, however, a different kind of swindle to the ones just enumerated, and is so well known to the reading public that any minute description of how the "oracle is worked" is unnecessary

One man may by himself run a "long firm" Adroitness in laying plans, address in approaching victims, general knowledge of business and money-matters, and a gullible public, are the essential requisites in this branch of professional crime. They are usually well-conducted men in prison; and I have found numbers of them to have once had an honest calling or business at some period in early life, and to have drifted by natural bent, or perhaps failure in their first pursuits, into a life of dishonest adventure. They are all mockers of religion, and, of course, regardless of truth or honour in their conversation or dealings with others. One of them may be taken as a type of the whole class.

During the two last years of my detention in Dartmoor, I was in daily labour companionship with one of these professional swindlers, and I have listened to many an account of his exploits upon what he styled the "ignorance and cupidity of the public." His father had been a schoolmaster in

VOL. I. D

the army, and had given his son "Jerry" a very good education Ho, however, chose the military in preference to any other life, and ere long, owing to his good conduct and superior intelligence, was promoted to the rank of sergeant. Growing tired in a few years of barrack soldiering he was purchased out, and given a little mea .- with which to push his way in the business world Removing to London, he soon squandered the few pounds that had been given to him by his fa. , and being very averse to earning a livelihood by manual labour, he fell back upon his wits, and began to run a "long firm" In this he was most successful for a time, and acquired sufficient money to get married and live in furnished lodgings; his wife being, according to his apparently truthful account, an honest person, who believed herself to be marrying a city clerk when she took "Jerry" for better or worse His plan of operation was simplicity itself; a plan which he declared would not have succeeded if those whose goods it brought to his "office" or "warehouse," did not believe they were about to obtain "a dishonest profit" out of their new London customers In fact he simply termed it "a game of rogue catch rogue," or diamond cut diamond He would forward advertisements to several provincial papers, purporting to relate to a business or agency carried on in the City of London,

whereby respectable manufacturers, farmers, &c., in the
country could dispose of their goods at large profits, if
saleable in London ; if otherwise, by shipment to the
colonies, or other places abroad. Cattle dealers, grain
growers, &c, could also be accommodated, and have
their stock disposed of for a moderate commission
Satisfactory references if required. Terms cash, on
receipt of goods for shipment or London market. By
renting a few cheap rooms in different parts of the city,
forging "satisfactory testimonials," and prompt dis-
appearance from such of his "offices" as were honoured
with goods, and a constant change of plans, "Jerry"
succeeded in evading the vigilance of the authorities
for a considerable time. He was captured at last,
however, fortunately for himself, in some trifling
swindle, and without being identified with any of his
previous transactions, he was sentenced to twelve
months' imprisonment. Upon his release he immediately set about running an insurance company, by
which, however, he failed to acquire any considerable
amount, owing to several such frauds having been
exposed by the police a short time previously. Arrested
again upon a charge of obtaining some clothing on
false pretences, he succeeded so well in his defence
that he was acquitted for want of full incriminating
evidence. This escape happened while I was awaiting
my trial in Newgate, and among the prisoners with

whom I had to exercise while detained in that prison
was "Jerry," who, on this ground, claimed a prison
acquaintanceship with me when he was afterwards
caught again, sentenced to seven years' penal servitude,
and confined in Dartmoor. Within one week after the
failure to convict him just alluded to, he carried out
successfully the following swindle, which, for coolness
of execution and originality of selection in the important matter of a victim, is perhaps unsurpassed by
any previous artist in a similar profession. He deliberately walked one day into the Home Office, and
requested an interview with the Secretary of State,
who at that time was Mr. B——, now Lord A——.
On this being accorded, "Jerry" represented himself
as a waiter from Willis's, and as having been sent by
a gentleman staying there, who was one of Mr. B—— s
constituents from A——shire. He, the gentleman, had
come up to London on business a few days previously,
and had unconsciously emptied himself of all his cash
in the business transactions referred to, and found
himself, when on point of departure home, without
what would either pay his hotel bill, or purchase a
railway ticket. To borrow money from those with
whom he had dealt might injure his credit, and
acquaintances he had none in London. It occurred to
him in this dilemma that he was a constituent of
Mr. B——'s; and as he had voted for him at the last

election, he might venture to apply to him for the loan of what would extricate him from this little difficulty, which, of course, would be returned immediately on his arrival home. A card with a name and an address was then handed to the Home Secretary by the reputed waiter, which, together with the story told by "Jerry," seemed so satisfactory to Mr. B—— that he expressed his gladness to be able to serve a constituent thus situated. On looking into his purse, Mr. B—— exclaimed, "By Jove, I have not enough change about me. Would a cheque for 10*l*. answer, think you?" "The gentleman only bid me ask for 8*l*.," replied the astute "Jerry," "and I think he would prefer having it in change." Whereupon the Home Secretary called a clerk from a desk, borrowed the requisite amount, and handed it to "Jerry." "I felt quite proud of this exploit," remarked "Jerry," when relating it, "to think of the second important individual in the Government being done by me, and in the Home Office too!"

On another occasion he presented himself at one of the principal travelling-bag and portmanteau dealing establishments in Piccadilly, and inquired if the Marquis of Lorne had called there that afternoon and made a purchase? "No; his lordship had not honoured them with a visit," "Jerry" was told, and at once he became the recipient of all possible deferential attention from the shopman "Strange," replied "Jerry" "His grace the duke told me that the marquis or his purchase might be found here," with which exclamation he left the place. Returning on the following day he handed the attendant, to whom he had spoken the previous day, a paper upon which he had written, in what he styled "an aristocratic scrawl," the following order.— " Messrs. ——, Piccadilly. Please send me, per bearer, two of your fifty-guinea travelling cases for purpose of selecting one to suit, and forward bill for same, and oblige.—ARGYLL." " So eager," remarked " Jerry," " are London dealers to be patronised by the nobility, that I have always found it comparatively easy to swindle them. In this instance, not only did they not consider the fact that the Duke of Argyll, or any such person of consequence, would never make a purchase in such a manner, but the shopman used his best endeavours to send articles worth 80*l*., instead of the prices stipulated, and was most anxious to be allowed to forward the bill at some future time. Such obsequious flunkeyism," concluded " Jerry," " deserved to be cheated. 1 walked off with the two bags, and netted 25*l*. by the transaction." " Jerry " was afterwards surprised in trying on a somewhat similar dodge in the matter of a gold chronometer, and was awarded seven years' penal servitude for what swindling of his had been detected by the police.

He was exceedingly attached to his wife, who did not repudiate him upon discovering his manner of obtaining a livelihood; and her letters to him while he was in Dartmoor were full of earnest implorings to abandon his former pursuits when his sentence would expire. I was compelled to feel some interest in him owing to many traits in his character which went to show that all was not bad in the man, and from the belief that he might possibly be induced to lead an honest life after being liberated. Being discharged on ticket-of-leave a few weeks previous to my own unexpected liberation, I sought him out a little while after my arrival in London, and found all the statements he had made to me, in relation to his wife and other personal matters, to have been correct. "I promised you," he exclaimed upon meeting me, "that I would live 'on the square' in future, and here is evidence of a commencement," showing at the same time a copy of the *Daily Telegraph* with an advertisement as follows:—"Wanted, two hundred barmaids." "That," remarked "Jerry," "is simply to arrest the attention of the fair sex, and cause them to read what follows. 'Extraordinary triumph of science! Marvellous results to health and complexion from the use of Fitzjerry's skin purifier. Freckles and disfiguring marks removed by one phial. To be had only of respectable druggists. Price 1s. 1½d. per phial. The

trade also supplied.   Prepared only by Fitzjerry, ——
Street, London'"   "Is this a real discovery, or merely
a quack nostrum?" I ventured to inquire, after reading
the above.   "Well, it is innocuous, at any rate," said
"Jerry," with a smile, "and that cannot be said of
most of such compounds   It possesses as much virtue
as any of the so-called remedies of a similar description
that are purchased in such large quantities by women,
who are adventurous enough to try and disguise their
years, or vain enough to add to their natural stock of
beauty. Thousands of men live well and honestly
upon the silliness and credulity of the fair sex, and
my elixir is not a particle more of a swindle than the
like preparations that are sold all over the country"
"Are you making much profit out of the article?" I
asked   "So far I have been doing very well," he
answered, "and hope to do better in the course of the
next few months, after which I may try my hand at
something else"   "How did you succeed in establish-
ing sufficiently the fame of your 'marvellous discovery'
to beget a prompt demand for it?   Was it by the mere
advertisement of its virtues?"   "Not altogether," he
replied, laughing, "but by the use of a little stratagem
I employed six young girls for one week at the rate of
10s. each, to perform the following additional advertisement   I assigned to each a certain district in this city,
in which every chemist's or druggist's shop was to be

visited by one after the other of the girls, and Fitz-jerry's purifier asked for This demand made six times in a few days would, in six cases out of ten, beget an order of at least a dozen phials from each druggist, leaving me a large profit upon every such order." "So this is what you call living honestly?" "Well, it is safe, anyhow," he rejoined, "and that is, with me, the next consideration to the one of profit. It is as near to honesty as I can go, as yet, and if I am fortunate in this business, I will improve upon its morality by and by."

I had the curiosity to try and see "Jerry" again some twelve months after this episode, and learn how he was getting along, but failed to discover any trace of him at his former residence, or place of business, and I very much fear that the strong natural propensity to live at the expense of the public in some surreptitious manner or other has overcome both good resolution and the deterrent fact of previous imprisonment, and landed "Jerry" once more within the walls of prison. I have, of course, disguised both the name of this individual, and the particular nature of his "honest venture," in the foregoing account of himself and the various schemes by which he played upon what he termed the "ignorance and cupidity of the public." But, with this exception, the remainder of this sketch is literally true.

I have dwelt at some length upon this type of the class of criminals belonging to the section of the best-conducted class of men in a convict prison, because an illustration of the character and schemes of one will apply more or less to the entire order of professional swindlers; and may, perhaps, be the means of warning gullible people against those arts and practices, the successful working of which encourages crime, and swells the penal roll of these countries

LECTURE IV.

THE remaining section of Class II, "snide pitchers"
(utterers of base coin), present very little of either originality in their plan of working, or ingenuity in the
exchange of their own for the coin of the realm. It
very rarely happens that "a maker" is caught, though
scores of them are known to carry on their profession in
London alone; while each large city in the country has
more or less numbers of such manufacturers. I only
knew one maker to be amongst the thousands of
convicts who came under my notice during my nine
years' experience of penal servitude, though it is of
course, possible that there may have been a larger
number in the various prisons in which I was from time
to time incarcerated. He was a very intelligent fellow,
very well behaved, who had done five years of a
"lagging" previous to his then sentence of ten years

In the same prison—Millbank—was a man who had purchased "snide" from the maker alluded to, and was caught in the act of attempting to pass some of it, and, though having no previous conviction against him, he was awarded fourteen years' penal servitude for this, his first offence. This appeared to me to be somewhat of a "slight mistake" in the administration of justice Both prisoners were tried at the same Newgate Sessions, but there was no connection between their cases.

As a rule, the "snide" dealers do not carry on any other species of swindle, nor do they resort to picking pockets, or burglary. Most of them are working men or servants out of employment. Very few make a boast of their particular crime, and I have invariably heard them resolve not to continue it any more after release They are not, as a rule, an intelligent order of men, but rank much higher in the scale of morality than criminals previously described. Publicans, and gullible people on racecourses, or at other betting places, are their favourite victims, with such other section of the public as chance may throw in their way for an exchange of coin. A little Frenchman who worked with me for a time in Dartmoor was an expert artist in this profession, and might have fared better in the matter of length of imprisonment, when ultimately captured, had some lenient teetotaller been his judge He made publicans almost his exclusive customers, and

always worked upon one plan, which he prided himself
upon being as simple as it had proved itself successful
on many occasions. With a stock of the best made
"snide," that is, cleverly counterfeited coin, with a fair
balance of genuine gold and silver in the make-up, he
would rush into a public-house or gin palace with head
bare, and pen behind the ear, and, as if he had just
slipped out of a neighbouring office or establishment, call
for a glass of beer or spirits, and pay the "damage"
with a half sovereign or half-a-crown, in a manner
that would as much as say "I have just run out from
my desk for this drink, and if I am not back in a
jiffy, old quill-driver, my employer, will be after me,
so please hurry up with the change" Of course a
great deal would depend upon the quality and make-
up of the article, gold being more difficult to pass than
silver; and excitement or presence of a large number
of people in a "public" being more conducive to an
easy "sell" than under calmer business circumstances

Another plan adopted by old hands is to tender a
genuine sovereign for payment of what is purchased,
and require the change to be in gold and silver; the
"snide" half sovereign is substituted by palming for
the good one which forms part of the change, and
is rung upon the counter with "Another instead of
this, if you please," demanded by the knowing customer.
Fairs and markets in the provinces are a favourite

resort for the snide pitchers, where they not unfrequently "take in" unsuspecting country dealers, as successfully as Moses Primrose was "sold" by the merchant of green spectacles in the *Vicar of Wakefield*.

LECTURE V.

CLASS III. MAGSMEN.

Crime included in this Class—What combines to make a Magsman—Tries to Deceive even Prison Officials—His Conduct
in Prison—Endeavours to Prey upon other Prisoners—His
" Religious " Dodges—He plays the Unfortunate " Aristocrat," the Neglected " British Soldier," &c —The Card
Sharper—The Three-card Trick Swindle explained.

CLASS III—This class is more diversified in the
criminal pursuits of its members than any other, save
number one, and forms the most troublesome, though
not the most violent or dangerous, body of men in a
convict prison. As they are almost all well known to
the police authorities when outside, they are in no way
anxious to obtain a ticket of leave. For this reason
they make very little effort while undergoing imprisonment to earn the quantity of marks, by good conduct
and performance of task, which entitle the well-conducted prisoner to the remission of a certain portion
of his sentence.

They may be divided into two sections: those who
employ their wits as weapons, and those who only use
their fingers against the public; or, to put it in slang
phraseology, "magsmen" and "hooks." The order of
magsmen will comprise card-sharpers, "confidence-
trick" workers, begging-letter writers, bogus ministers
of religion, professional noblemen, "helpless victims
of the cruel world," medical quacks, and the various
other clever rogues that figure from time to time
in the newspaper records of crime. It would require a volume to do justice to the character, tricks,
and peculiar physiognomy of this section alone. They
prey upon all classes, and have no more compunction
in "besting" one of themselves than in robbing out-
siders, while of all criminals they are the most consum-
mate hypocrites and accomplished liars   It is difficult
to determine whether nature or civilisation has done
most in developing the cheating propensity of the magsman   All the roguery and dishonesty that is begotten
of our boasted civilisation superinduced upon all that
is deceitful and unprincipled in depraved human
nature, would seem to unite in the finished production
of one of these rascals

He puts his professional talents into working gear
even in prison, and endeavours to get the blind side of
chaplain or priest by apparent sanctity and ready
Scriptural quotations; to cheat the doctor into admission

to the prison hospital by feigning sickness, and enu-
merating all the maladies that had preyed for years
upon all the members of his family; while he will even
carry his trickery so far—often too far for himself—as
to endeavour to impose upon the governor in the hope
of being able to shirk some particularly disagreeable
task, or to obtain admission into some light labour or
other privileged work gang.

Failing in any or all of these efforts; the magsman
becomes the constant grumbler of the prison establishment. He is up before the governor with complaints
as frequently as it is prudent to do so, and applies to
see the visiting director every month "to show up" the
warders for over-doing their duty, the prison baker for
under-doing the bread, the cook for making the skilly
or shin-of-beef soup too thin, or some other prisoner
for giving personal trouble or annoyance. When near-
ing the termination of his sentence the magsman will
endeavour to procure the addresses of friends belonging
to any prisoner who may have those outside who would,
if possible, lighten the burdens of their imprisoned
relatives. Should he succeed in obtaining the least
excuse for an introduction, the magsman will represent
himself as being in a position to transmit money to his
friend languishing in prison, "and thereby help to
lighten the remainder of his sentence by bribing warders
into a kind treatment of the poor suffering gentleman

who begged him (the magsman) not to forget his old prison chum when restored to liberty," &c. Several instances of this kind of swindle came under my notice while in Dartmoor, through prisoners' relatives writing particulars of them to those who had been stupid enough to aid in their perpetration.

Magsmen are, as a necessary consequence of their following, the most accomplished in the art of lying of all mortals; but, like all habitual liars or rogues, are very deficient in the important article of memory, and may be easily detected in the falsehood of their story or yarn by those who will but examine closely their narratives and purposes. Still it is easy to account for their swindling success by the knowledge of how prone many persons are to credit the artfully-invented and pathetically-related tales that are poured into their ears or penned for their perusal by an unfortunate "minister of the Gospel," at one time "happy in the Lord," and in the possession of a home for his weak family, but now "meekly bowing to the Divine chastisement in poverty," &c., &c.; or a disinherited son of an unforgiving wealthy parent, "who has been cast off without a shilling for having married below his station," or for the commission of some other offence against aristocratic caste or society rule, but "resolved to hide his ancestral name and family reputation from the scandal-loving public while seeking some assistance for his true and injured partner in life and children, pending happier smiles of fortune," &c.; or the touching appeal of "the ex-British soldier, maimed or otherwise injured whilst serving his country, chiefly in India, and now doomed to live upon the generosity of his countrymen, through an indiscretion by which a pension was lost," &c.; or the engaging manners, polite talk, and graciously-condescending deportment of the general, colonel, captain, or nobleman who is on a venture at a country hotel, or among those who dearly love the patronage of the upper ten.

It may seldom happen that a magsman is captured for a swindle exactly corresponding with the foregoing descriptions, as few people who find themselves gulled in such a manner care to figure in the public press as being the simpletons which they would have to be depicted in prosecuting a "minister," "baronet," "colonel," or any other sham who might have honoured them with a month's hospitality, or borrowed a paltry 50l. while awaiting a remittance from an estate agency or bank; but these exploits are of common occurrence, nevertheless, and form the boast of such of the magsman fraternity as successfully carry them out.

To put the people who are generally victimised by this type of rogue to some extent on their guard, it will be necessary to give a few particulars of their respective plans of operation.

One particular accomplishment is nearly common to all of them—they are admirable judges of character, and seldom fail in selecting the most credulous and otherwise work able individuals in a company, or in any other convenient circumstance, for the victim that is to be fleeced. This forms a necessary part of their profession, and as they make its practice an object of constant application they become clever physiognomists.

The Card-Sharper.—This artist, until recent enactments in his regard, was a frequenter of railway trains, and has often victimised young and inexperienced travellers by aid of the three-card trick, but he is now driven to other fields of operation, chiefly country towns and highways, sailor-frequented haunts at seaports, and low beer-shops. He is the least educated of the magsman order and will not scruple to pick an occasional pocket, or otherwise help himself to anything which fortune may throw in his way. In the preliminary to the introduction of his "two black and one red" game, his conversation will be almost certain to turn upon horse racing, pedestrianism, fortunes made on the turf, London or Manchester gaming-saloons; after which he finally comes to cards. If the game that follows is to be played in or near a town, confederates will figure in it. If on a country road, one professional will suffice. When two are "working the oracle," the usual plan is this: One will introduce

himself and the game to the company, or knot of men
or boys, as the case may be, in something like the
manner I have just described, and produce his pack of
cards, or three of a pack, two black and one red, or *vice
versâ*—this being the number needed for the game. At
this point of the proceedings the confederate will come
upon the scene and appear deeply interested in the
game. The man with the cards offers to bet any
gentleman a "tanner" that he will not pick the red
card out from the two black ones, which he shuffles
Still spe..."ng, he throws down upon a table, board, or
any such object that he may be near, his three cards.
The confederate appears very desirous of accepting the
challenge—hesitates, seeks advice from the person next
to him, declares that a certain card to which he points
must be the right one, and finally throws down sixpence, puts his finger upon the card, and obtai... the
wager. With much ado on the part of the owner of
the cards, the successful speculator is induced to bet
again, which he reluctantly does, and wins; again, and
loses this time, and once more for an augmented wager
(the confederate appearing to warm to the sport) of
perhaps five "bob" (shillings), and wins. By this
time some of the lookers-on will be induced, by what
they have seen, to stake a small sum, when they
will, of course, be allowed to win, until, sufficiently
excited to increase their wagers, it becomes worth

the sharper's while to turn the winning on his own side

The manner in which the trick is performed is as follows. The card-sharper holds two cards in the palm of the right hand and one in that of the left; the front one of the former will be the red, and will be held so as to be plainly seen by the audience, and the other two will be the black ones. One of the latter—the one held in the right hand behind the red—will be cut perhaps the sixteenth of an inch shorter than the other two, so that it can be thrown *from behind the red*, when the cheat is to be performed, into a space on the table or board where the red appears to, and should, fall, if the game were honestly played; while the red remains the last card in the right hand, and is thrown where the black one should fall. When the victim is being induced to speculate he will observe the red card pitched to the right or left, and the two others thrown so that the three will o face downwards in something like the form of a triangle. As the red will be purposely shown, in the first instance, when flung from the sharper's hand, the speculator will, of course, be able to pick it out from the other two, until he wagers the larger amount, when the red is, as usual, exposed while apparently falling as before, and the black one that is behind it in the sharper's hand is easily flung into the place where the red had previously been thrown, the red relegated to the unsuspected position, and the cheat accomplished.

An experienced hand at this game will be "fly" enough not to win continuously when he gets his victim or victims fully engaged in the speculation, but will allow an occasional victory to be scored against him, so as neither to excite the suspicion of trickery, nor to discourage the interested spectators.

The foregoing particulars of this well-known cheat, anything but well known in its manner of being worked, was given me by one who was admitted by his criminal friends to be especially smart in this branch of a magsman's profession. He boasted, among other similar achievements, of having "emptied" a young Etonian of his gold watch and 20*l* while travelling with his dupe on the short journey from London to Windsor

This type of criminal is of the hardened species, and is quite irreclaimable, while he ranks the first in the downward course from the class of "honourable thieves"

LECTURE VI

CLASS III.   MAGSMEN (*continued*).

The "Confidence" Trick Swindle explained

THIS cheat is such a transparent "sell" that it excites
one's astonishment how any mortal is allowed to wander
abroad in the world by himself who is capable of being
fleeced by its agency.

I will stake my reputation for knowledge of national
character that a Jew, a Dutchman, a Yankee, or a Scot,
never lost a farthing by means of this most shallow of
all artful dodges; yet how many individuals have figured
in the police columns of the press (in my opinion deservedly thus pilloried for their asinine stupidity) as
prosecutors in such cases!

A "gowk" (countryman)   generally the quarry for
whose capture the workers of this little game are
always on the alert   The vicinity of the Tower, British
Museum, St. Paul's, and other London sights that attract
the curious and country-cousin type of visitors to the

metropolis, are the most frequent beats of these professors, who are never at a loss to discover their prey owing to the gaping and wonder-at-everything looks of the provincials. The successful performance of the swindle requires two or more confederates, who will keep in sight of each other while on the look-out for game, but who will pass and repass each other while thus occupied as if utter strangers. When an intended victim is selected, he is approached by one of the rogues and asked for some information as to the direction towards, or locality of a certain street, hotel, theatre, &c., the inquirer using such deferential bearing as the apparent wealth or weakness of the victim may invite; stating at the same time that he (the rogue) is a perfect stranger in London, arrived that day from some very remote part of the country, and is completely lost in the surrounding wilderness of stone and mortar He will, of course, be answered by the real stranger, that he is from the country also, and can give no such information; whereupon a conversation is started, an adjournment to a public-house proposed, and a drink invited—the rogue respectfully requesting the pleasure of treating "the only gentleman who has given him a civil answer since his arrival in London." If this is agreeable to the sight-seer, the nearest low tavern or beershop is selected for the drink, and the game is all but bagged. If the beershop should be a rendezvous for thieves, the robbery becomes quite easy. The stranger's second drink is drugged, his pockets rifled, and himself left to awake a poorer but a wiser man But if it be an ordinary or respectable establishment, the operation of "maggin the gowk out of his purse" becomes less certain; depending, principally, upon the amount of ignorance which he has carried with him to London, and on the acting and conversational "confidence-inspiring" powers of the gentleman into whose hands he has fallen. While the new acquaintance are in the act of drinking each other's health, the confederate makes his appearance, with an "I hope I am not intruding, gentlemen," and sets about the work of obtaining a closer introduction to the company In the meantime rogue 1 has baited the trick by exhibiting some "Bank of Engraving" notes, and a flash, well-filled purse of "snide," or gilt coin, out of which he will have taken a genuine half-sovereign with which to pay for the treat; remarking, at the same time, in reference to the amount of supposed money just exhibited, "that a man cannot come to London to enjoy himself, you know, without putting a few pounds of spending money in his pocket."

The turn which the conversation will now take must mainly depend on chance, the two rogues, however, measuring their victim both as to his comparative

clownishness and financial condition. Pending the
introduction of the business portion of the confidence
comedy, rogue 2 will launch out against London dishonesty in general, and declare that he is compelled
to put his purse and watch under his pillow in the
hotel where he is staying, and to carry the former in
his breast-pocket when walking in the streets, for fear
of losing both, winding up with the regret that he
could place no confidence whatever in these Londoners
Rogue 1 admits the unfortunate lax morality of a
great number of people in such a large city, but
ventures an opinion that a stranger to the metropolis
may allow his prejudice or imagination to conjure up
dishonesty where none really existed; and that want
of confidence in everybody would beget a miserable
state of things, and a want of confidence in one's own
judgment and common sense among the number. All
this time the stranger is but called upon to act the
part of a listener, the two rogues carrying on the
discussion, and paying for the drink consumed, until
eventually rogue 1 carries the argument against his
adversary, and declares his willingness to intrust his
purse and contents to either rogue 2 or the other
gentleman during a period of five or ten minutes'
absence from the room, and without requiring any
other guarantee for the safe return of his property
beyond his own confidence in their observed honour

and honesty   Rogue 2 declares this to be handsome on
the part of the gentleman who speaks, but thinks that
prudence, as well as the observed customs of business
transactions, demand that the party in whom such
trust is reposed should not accept it without leaving
some pledge of his honour in the hands of the confiding gentleman. Therefore, he, rogue 2, will take
up the challenge of rogue 1, providing he (rogue 1)
will take the custody of his purse until he (the speaker)
comes back; requesting, however, the company of the
other gentleman, the stranger, while he is absent from
the room. This course is agreed to by the man of
confidence, and the purses are exchanged. The parties
absenting themselves return, of course, at the end of
the stipulated time, and the first act of the comedy
is performed   Another drink, this time at the expense of rogue 2, who insists on treating the gentleman
who had honoured him with such confidence, and a
similar performance is enacted by rogue 2 declaring
that he will not be outdone in the exhibition of
confidence , and purses are again exchanged between
the confederates, rogue 1 being the volunteer absentee
in this act, accompanied by the gentleman, his friend
from the country. The second act over, it comes to
the dupe's turn to show his confidence in one
of the two "gentlemen," whereupon the rogue who
obtains the custody of the purse vanishes with it, is

gone in search of by his friend when the time expires and the dupe is left alone with the flash purse filled with threepence-worth of gilt sovereigns, and with plenty of food for reflection upon the silly goose he has made of himself.

This confidence trick does not constitute a profession in itself: it is simply one of the accomplishments of a magsman, and may be performed by a card-sharper or any other artist who belongs to the magsman order of professional criminals.

LECTURE VII.

CLASS III.   MAGSMEN (*continued*).

The Begging-Letter Wr...—His Demeanour in Convict society
—His College Day... How Managed by the Governor—The
Begging-Letter Writer's Accomplishments—Knowledge of
Aristocratic Scandal—How he Lays his Plans—How Executed
—Injury done by these Frauds to the Deserving Respectable
Poor—"*The Sanctimonious Fraud*"—Real Ministers of the
Gospel in Prison—Their usual Crime—The Sham Minister
—His Account of Himself—His "Misfortunes"—Sectarian
Animosity supplies the Bogus Divine with his Field of
Operation—The un-Christian Character of this Feeling—
"The Rev" Mr Blank—His Conversion to Catholicity—
Re-conversion to Protestantism

BEGGING-LETTER WRITERS.—These are "the people
of quality" in a prison, and, together wit' "the scions
of the nobility," to be described by and by, constitute
the would-be *crême de la crême* of its society I have
passed many an amusing half hour, during Sunday
exercise, in simply observing the walk, bearing, and
aristocratic airs assumed by these individuals, and
have often had to listen to their stories of "family

intrigue," "fortunes lost on the turf," &c, &c, by
means of which the narrators were ruined, and consigned to prison by unscrupulous relatives, or through
the mad follies of youth and pleasure They never
admit their real calling when in conversation with
other prisoners, but invariably represent themselves
as belonging to good families in society, by whom,
or some members of which, or by their own freaks,
they have been ruined. But in order to screen the
family name from the reproach of having had a representative a convict, they have assumed another name
as a *nom de prison*, &c., &c. When it is safe to do
so they put on airs too, and look down upon the
thieves who are honest enough to avow their professional pursuit, and who, in their turn, treat their
soi-disant superiors as an Arab would handle a Jew,
or with something like the contempt that a South
Carolina planter of the old school would listen to the
family pedigree of a gentleman "of colour." Whether
they need them or not, these amusing frauds will
exhaust all the forms of a prison to obtain a pair of
spectacles. These adjuncts to intellectual physiognomy
lend an air of respectability and learning to their
wearers, and assist them in the *rôle* which they are
desirous to sustain among their convict associates. As
a rule they are a troublesome type of men for prison
officials to deal with, exceedingly averse to anything

approaching hard labour, but having a similar detestation for the diminution of rations served to men at minor laborious tasks. They are consequently known among other prisoners as "doctor's and governor's men"—that is, men who are constantly complaining and seeking favours or more agreeable forms of occupation They are eventually relegated to some sedentary employment, such as tailoring, shoe-making, or stocking-knitting, where they pass the remainder of their imprisonment in the enjoyment of their reputed family distinction and respectable belongings in the outer world

The governor and other superior prison officials have, of course, a thorough knowledge of criminal character, and know how to deal with each class and type in the manner most conducive to the maintenance of prison discipline Every prisoner is privileged to see the governor whenever he has a complaint to make, or a reasonable application to submit; but a too frequent exercise of this privilege upon trivial or ridiculous excuses, is, of course, provocative of annoyance, and a source of unnecessary trouble to the prison staff. I have known the governor to have "choked off" (successfully humbugged) dozens of these frequently complaining and contemptible impostors by expressing his surprise at "*an educated man* giving such trouble without cause"—a compliment which was, of course,

related to every individual who came within talking
distance of the recipient during the remainder of his
"lagging." They are a very well-informed class of
men, as a rule; numbers of them having received
portions of legal or other professional education; while
ex-schoolmasters, broken - down tutors, " spoiled "
ministers, and questionable lawyers are found among
their number They are all past middle age Most of
them will have undergone short terms of imprisonment,
before entering upon convict life, not necessarily for
having been guilty of the begging-letter fraud, but for
that or any of the other swindles already or hereafter
to be specified as belonging to the general profession of
a magsman. They will not pick pockets, or undertake
burglary, but will work a bogus insurance company,
run a long firm, or engage in any similar undertaking
Should several of them meet in one " push " (labour
party) in a prison, they will aid each other in the
support of their assumed rank, and speak of " that
unfortunate poor devil, register No A 2,000, who
squandered a fortune on the turf, or in Baden-Baden ,
or who moved in good society the time *I* first made his
acquaintance, a few years after I had graduated in
Cambridge, &c , &c " They are easily distinguished
among the mass of other prisoners, not altogether by
their airs or their " distinguished extraction," but chiefly
from what constitutes their stock conversation, namely,

the pedigrees and concerns of the English and Scotch nobility. There is scarcely a member of the House of Lords or other titled personage in Great Britain whose family history, particulars of wild freaks of male, or *faux pas* of female members, and general scandal thereto belonging, I have not listened to in my Sunday and daily exercises in Dartmoor, from members of the begging-letter fraternity. This intimate knowledge of the family doings of the upper ten of society is the essential part of the begging-letter impostor's profession, without which he would be no more capable of swindling in his peculiar line than would a man who had never been to sea be able to regulate the rigging of a merchantman. This education acquired, by the study of works on the peerage, regular perusal of the fashionable intelligence columns of the daily papers and from other kindred sources, the fraud is perpetrated in something like the following manner :—

We will suppose that one of these characters has just read in the *Court Journal*, or other aristocratic organ, an item like the following "Fashionable marriage at St. James's, Hanover Square, on the 20th instant. The Honourable Gustavus Fitzswell, son of Viscount Fitzswell, of Berks, to Georgina Eleanor Victoria, eldest daughter of Sir Eustace Moneybags, of Grosvenor Square, London" Here follows, of course, the list of those present at the marriage ceremony, and

of all whom Sir Eustace entertained at breakfast or
lunch with the bride and bridegroom; particulars of
presents given to the bride; and the usual piece of
interesting intelligence "the happy couple left by an
early train for Torquay," or somewhere else, "there to
spend the honeymoon."

This paragraph is to the begging-letter writer what a
surface indication is to a gold-seeker on the Rocky
Mountains, or an unsuspecting country visitor to London
with plenty of spending money and lots of "confidence"
to the professional who gives lessons in that branch
of education for an exchange of purses. The paragraph is immediately copied on a slip of paper, three-
pence invested in writing materials, and the scene
changes to some miserable room in an upper story of
some lodging-house in Drury Lane, Whitechapel, or
Soho, in London. A greasy well-thumbed book is
diligently looked through in search of the names
"Fitzswell" and "Moneybags," and also for those
of such distinguished personages or people of wealth
who may have been among Sir Eustace's guests, and
the various particulars of the family history of each
will be diligently read over and committed to memory,
after which the interested student will carefully lay his
plans, and proceed to work. He may fix upon either of
the happy pair, or both, or their (of course) no less
happy parents; or some one of the guests, or half

a dozen, as his game ; circumstances determining both
the extent of and particular plan for accomplishing
the intended swindle. A carefully-worded letter is
written that will detail a distressing story of some
unfortunate mishap as having occurred in connection
with sickness and the loss of business, situation, patronage, or previous respectable occupation of the writer;
entailing, in consequence, great hardship upon himself,
his wife, and a very young family The principal misfortune may be represented as having resulted from
failure in business, after the retirement from the service
of some of the families concerned in the recent marriage
(names and particulars being added), or from being
deprived of the position of steward, footman, valet, &c.,
through some trifling fault, age, or other mitigating
circumstance Another start in business is contemplated:
the nature of which will be explained, and his recent
mistress or master, or both, have kindly and generously
headed the following list with a donation of 5*l.* Names
and amounts of donations will then be added, an address
given, and an intimation tendered that the smallest
help will be gratefully acknowledged, and the letter
is forwarded to its destination Care will, of course, be
taken not to send the list of generous "donations" to
any party whose name already figures thereon, while
the appeal will be made as respectable, pathetic, and
genuine-like as possible

Instead of a marriage, the inspiring paragraph may have referred to a party of guests entertained at some nobleman's or merchant's residence in the country—a dinner after a hunt, or other such usual occurrence in connection with the world of wealth or fashion

The writer may elect to hint himself a distant relative of some of the personages taking part in the particular event that has brought such people together, and in making a genteel appeal, lay special stress upon the point that he would a thousand times prefer taking his wife and children into an almshouse than that his relative, Ge¹, Colonel, or Captain Somebody, or the member for Stonehenge, should hear of the means to which he was compelled to resort to keep his family from starving

Scores of other devices are employed by this fraternity in preying upon feelings of human sympathy, which, in consequence of such criminal practices, are often steeled against genuine and deserving domestic or individual suffering, or the alleviation of helpless poverty.

Numbers of these magsmen travel through the country, and by intercourse with servants in large houses, and listening to the gossip of village inns, are enabled to carry on a safer, and probably more profitable, "business," than that pursued by the city

ofessors of the same calling. Another species present
themselves in person to known charitable people in
cities and towns, and by artful representations and an
exhibition of the list already apparently patronised
with small contributions, succeed in defrauding the
open-hearted and generous.

So long as human pity is capable of being put in
motion by the calamities that are incidental to the
lives of the unfortunate, these begging-letter impostors
will be more or less successful in their depredations
upon society, and one is therefore far from desiring
anything like a crusade against even unconscionable
ias that would be likely to involve the honest
needy and really afflicted in an undisciminating
suspicion and repudiation at the hands of the pub .

Sanctimonious Frauds—This class of crime is not
largely re esented in convict society, but I have been
informed that it is oftener found in county prisons, and
is usually associated with the preceding and kindred
species of swindling I regret to have to say that I
have known several *bona fide* ministers of religion who
were convicts, their crime, as a general rule, being
bigamy, but as they are not a type of habitual criminal,
nor their special offence one of a recurring nature, I
have grouped them in the first section of Class I
Their presence in any branch of criminal life or class of
prison association is a sad commentary upon the morals

of modern society, and has often supplied an apposite argument to those of the intelligent, irreformable offenders, who love to scoff at the idea of an honest or moral principle regulating the co⁻ⁱ⁻⁻ or guiding the motives, of any portion of civilise   kind

The bogus divine might be termed a religious *chevalier d'industrie.* He has probably a better verbal knowledge of Scripture than many a surpliced occupant of a pulpit, with a face capable of expressing such a degree of unctuous piety as would do credit to the most fervid enthusiast at a religious love-feast As the lay members of his (the magsman's) profession prey upon the simple and inexperienced amongst sinners, the sacerdotal impostor selects his victims from amongst the over-credulous portion of saints The presence of that unfortunately too generally infused " Christian charity," which the poet has aptly termed " the hating of each other for the love of God,' is the source of this among the many other evils which flow from the religious animosities of rival sects The most hardened sinner that eve repudiated or trampled upon the whole decalogue by sinful and scandal-giving conduct is not one-hundredth part as welcome to " the path of repentance "—be it within the fold of church, chapel, or meeting house—as the Scripture-searching, conscience-troubled individual who has discovered some flaw in the theology or innovation in the ceremonial of his previously acknowledge religion, and who declares he has at last found out and elected to follow "the true path" This blind zeal in behalf of sect is believed by those who manifest it to be a laudable thing in the interests of true religion, and is, of course, common to all Christian denominations, without exception, and therefore opens up an extensive field for those adepts in simulated sanctit, ' converted truth-seekers," and "reformed divines," some of whom are occasionally found in a convict prison

Like the begging-letter writer, the "converted minister" is (to his prison auditors) "of good family extraction," had, at least, a college education, and has either been awfully sinned against by wicked men, or has fallen into his present prison misfortune through some cause which requires the relation of his whole family history, or personal mistakes, to explain Anything approaching to a truthful statement of what they really did to get into prison it is impossible to learn from their own lips.

Like the individuals previously sketched, these divine magsmen aid each other in the support of their fictitious characters while in prison, and talk of such a prisoner being a Cambridge man, and such another as having taken honours at Oxford, while some other has been a chaplain in the army. One of these most accomplished rogues introduced himself to me one day in Dartmoor (it having happened that accident threw us together at exercise) and afforded me a half hour's amusement. "An extraordinary deputation, consisting of several M P.'s, and other influential gentlemen, waited upon the Home Secretary last week," he at onc gan, "and made use of the following argument in _y behalf:— 'Sir, we, in common with the rest of the public, have observed how much the Government has done towards the liberation of the Fenian prisoners, with which leniency we entirely agree, but we have watched in vain for anything being done on behalf of the Rev Mr Blank, whose case excited so much interest a few years ago in London society We trust, therefore, sir, that his hitherto unblemished reputation, the fact that his offence was not of a nature to injure public orals, and the three years' confinement he has alread, underg gone, together with the deep sympathy that is felt for him by a wide section of intimate friends, will soon earn for him at your hands that considerate remission of sentence which has lately stored so many other prisoners to their families and friends' Yes, sir," he added, "I expect my discharge will be brought down by the visiting director next month, as the Government cannot afford to slight such an extra-ordinary deputation"

"Are you the rev person that is interceded for ?' I inquired

' Yes I was convicted for the alleged destruction of some title-deeds to property — a ridiculous supposition, as the papers would have established my own indisputable claim to what had been in the possession of my family for generations."

"Where did you officiate as priest ? "

"Oh ! I was a minister of the Established Church," he replied

"Then why do you attend the Catholic chapel, here ? " I asked

"Well," he answered, "I could not bear the preaching of the Protestant chaplain in — — rison, and I was ordered one day by an assistant — — 'or to *kneel down on both knees,* so I saw the director, and became a Catholic"

Cutting off one's nose to spite the remainder of the face is nothing in comparison to a man changing from a Protestant to a Catholic in order to save his knees A few months after the conversation just alluded to I missed his reverence from the Catholic chapel, where he had been a regular weekly communicant, as well as member of the convict choir, and upon exercising my curiosity as to what had become of him when I next had a visit from Father Green, I learned that the Rev Mr. Blank had again troubled the director in a matter of conscience, and had become a Protestant once more. " Because," remarked Father Green, "I had refused to recommend him to the governor for employment in the prison bakehouse !" Until the expiration of hi sentence Blank was a constant monthly communicant and a member of the choir in the Protestant, as he had just previously been in the Catholic, chapel I further learned from a prisoner who had been tried d convicted at the same sessions as Blank, that, instead of his having been "rigged" as a minister or gentleman previous to conviction, an "old clo' man" would not have speculated two and sixpence upon his entire outfit

These impostors' conduct in prison is a counterpart of the game which such swindlers carry on outside They are sufficiently conversant in Catholic, Protestant, and Presbyterian creeds to adopt either when money or free quarters can be obtained thereby. One can well picture the sensation which "a converted priest," or hitherto "spiritually benighted Papist," would create in any of those religious circles in Great Britain where the Pope and the Catholic Church are looked upon as the "beast" and the "scarlet lady" of the Scriptures. The collection of small silver that would follow "the confessions," and the "marks of earnest repentance of the convert" who had "at last found Christ," would be readily and ungrudgingly given to, and in all meekness pocketed by, the rogue, who next week, perhaps, would select his victims from some gullible section of

Catholics, who would del ... listenr. to ...
exposé of the characters of those who were instrumental in effecting the Reformation. A comparison
being instituted between either the devil or anti-
Christ and Martin Luther, would lose the pious magsman nothing on the occasion of this second collection

The bogus divine will work the begging-letter
dodge occasionally, or resort to frauds of a similar
nature but will not pick pockets, or do ordinary
vulgar thieving

LECTURE VIII.

BOGUS NOBLEMEN,

"Sir Roger Tichborne"—The Claimant's advent to Dartmoor society—His Status therein—A recognised Authority on all matters—His Insubordination—Difference between his conduct and that of self-acknowledged Shams—His knowledge of French and acquaintance with Catholic Ritual—Samples of his Political Education—Dr Kenealy's reference to the Claimant's Classical Knowledge—Another explanation—Impressions made upon Prisoners—The Claimant's explanation of the cowardly attack upon a lady witness—Charges the Jesuits with his ruin.

If the individual who has become a historical character under the cognomen of the "Claimant" be really Arthur Orton or Thomas Castro, he stands at the very head of his profession. If not, or rather, in any case, he is "an unfortunate nobleman," and comes naturally within this section of the classification I have made of a convict prison's roll. Although it is no concern of these brief sketches of criminal life and character whether the Claimant be Orton, Castro, or

Roger Tichborne, still, a few remarks upon his prison conduct, as observed by me during the two years he was a fellow-prisoner of mine in Dartmoor, may not be altogether out of place in passing.

I may remark, at the outset, that I have not read the great trial which resulted in his conviction as an impostor, nor am I in possession of any facts relative thereto, or particulars of the individual's life previous to such trial, that would enable me to form a just opinion whether he is the victim of conspiring circumstances, or, as he alleges, treachery, or a deservedly punished criminal.

His arrival in Dartmoor, after completing the usual probationary period in Millbank Penitentiary, created unusual excitement among both warders and prisoners, but particularly among the latter. "Sir Roger" soon became the lion of the place. To fall into exercising file with him on Sunday was esteemed an event to be talked of for a week afterwards by the fortunate convict, who had, for once in his life, rubbed his skirts against one of England's proud aristocracy. To settle an argument upon any topic—legal, political, or disciplinary—required but the assertion, "Sir Roger Tichborne says so," and an immediate acquiescence in the conclusiveness of the facts or opinions advanced was the consequence. In fact, "Sir Roger" soon became the recognised authority upon every matter f mome.. .o the on... ...... citizens of Dartmoor's

...nal population, from the merits of the skilly to
the evils of trial by jury, or from the partisanship of
judges to the quality of the shin-of-beef soup; and
the ... .tion to that secluded and unique society of
such a man was put down among the list of great
events in the history of Dartmoor. He remained the
standard authority upon juries, judges, money, and
victims of circumstantial evidence, to the whole chorus
of gossiping magsmen, until he was finally removed to
another prison.

He very soon became what prison officials term "a
troublesome prisoner" in Dartmoor, thereby ranking
himself among the class of criminals whom I have
placed in that category; and like all other convicts
who offended against the rules and regulations, he had
to undergo the penalty of bread-and-water diet, but
never for more than two, and very seldom but for one,
day at a time.

As his being a troublesome prisoner is one circumstance, though a very trivial one, towards an identity
between him and the "professional noblemen" with
whom I have classified him, it is but just to notice
another feature in his conduct which is never found in
connection with that of one of the magsman nobility.
Unlike the ordinary bogus aristocrat, "Sir Roger"
never "flashed his rank"—that is, when he walked

or talked with other prisoners, he did not "put on airs," or adopt the patronising manners that both outside, as well as in prison, usually denote alike the *parvenu* and the impostor He maintained his position, though, as the real "Sir Roger Tichborne" whenever brought before governor or visiting director, or when the fact might be questioned by other prisoners, and in his letters to outside friends while in Dartmoor. Whatever the man really is, victim or fraud, Tichborne or Castro, he exhibited, while under my observation, an individuality and a bearing in marked contrast to the ordinary impostors and criminals with whom he was associated.

I have been informed, that when questioned, during his trial, as to the meaning of certain French words, and particulars of some points in the Catholic faith, which the real Sir Roger, it is alleged, would be almost certain to know, he was unable to answer correctly in either case, thereby exhibiting his ignorance of a language spoken and the ritual of a creed professed by the legitimate Tichborne when at Stonyhurst. If this be correct, the Claimant must have acquired a knowledge both of French and the observances of the Mass in the interval between his conviction in London and his arrival in Dartmoor—a brief period of nine months—as he could both converse in French and correctly follow the ceremony of the Catholic Church

while in that prison. On the other hand, it is quite
possible that these parts in the *rôle* that was to be
played may have been studied during his nine months'
sojourn in Millbank, as Catholic books of devotion and
a French grammar and dictionary would be included,
if desired, among his ordinary cell books, while undergoing his probation in the penitentiary. Still, it is but
just to remark that few individuals are to be found
among convicts who could make such progress in
the study of a language which, though it be an easy
task to learn to read it, is seldom so easily mastered as
to enable a student to converse freely with a Frenchman at the expiration of nine months' self-tuition
On the other hand, Sir Roger's intellectual training
and extent of general knowledge, as far as could be
gathered from his prison conversation, appeared to
me to be far too limited for a man that was reputed to
have received a good college education, and who had,
in addition, travelled so much and mixed with so many
men the world over, and who had also the advantage of
having passed his forty-fifth year Dr Johnson's remark
upon the law of primogeniture that its chief excellence
consisted in only making one fool in a family, may, of
course, apply to the foregoing observations regarding
' Sir Roger's" ability; but without some such explanation it would be very difficult to account for his
many deficiencies in this respect and singular observa-

tions upon ordinary English topics, supposing him to
be the man he represents himself Having accidentally
heard the result of the general election of 1874, I com-
municated to "Roger" the triumph of the Tories and
the fact of Mr. Disraeli becoming Prime Minister;
whereupon he remarked, 'Then you see if he does not
make himself First Lord of the Treasury also" On
another occasion he informed me that Dr. Kenealy had
introduced *a bill* into the House of Commons the
week previously regarding his ("Roger's") treatment
in Dartmoor, when Dr. Kenealy had simply asked a
question of the Home Secretary in reference thereto.
His political knowledge appeared to be exactly on
a level with that of the ordinary magsman These
trifles may explain nothing as to the real character of
the individual of whom they are related, as every
Englishman is not supposed to have the correct use
of all the technical phrases of his country's somewhat
mixed political terminology; but they are mentioned
here as fair samples of the manner in which "Roger"
was in the habit of expressing himself upon such
matters and topics as intelligent men will make
subjects of conversational intercourse

Dr Kenealy is reported to have laid considerable
stress upon the testimony of a Latin quotation which
occurred in one of his client's letters from Dartmoor,
declaring, with a deal of truth, that the Wapping

butcher would not be likely to repeat lines from Horace in his epistolary productions; *ergo*, the man who did so was not Castro. The lines were—

" *Feliciter artes didicisse emollit mores*
Nec sinit esse feros,"

and form one of the most frequent stock classical quotations from the Latin poets that are to be met with, in company with their translation, throughout English literature. I have seen the same lines several times in prison library books in Dartmoor, and as the books of the prison are in constant circulation among the prisoners, it is almost certain that "Roger" would have come across one or other of the works in which I had read the lines referred to. *A propos* of this quotation, and the letter in which it was made, I was told by a very intelligent prisoner who had repeatedly conversed with "Roger," that the letter about the classical nature of which Dr. Kenealy sought to make so much capital for his client, was written for the latter by a prisoner with whom he ("Roger") was very intimate, and who passed himself off among his fellow-prisoners as "the heir-apparent to an earldom." I cannot vouch for the truth of the statement that the letter containing the lines of Horace was not "Roger's" production, and I merely relate it here as one of the many *on dits* that circulated concerning him among his fellow-prisoners while in Dartmoor.

The impression which he made upon nineteen out of every twenty prisoners with whom he was in daily contact while in Dartmoor was favourable to his claims and pretensions, but the sympathies of men who have imbibed and nourished a strong resentment to the law that has consigned themselves to penal servitude will almost always incline them to an adverse opinion of the fairness of its decision, and carry their prejudices to the side of " the innocent victims of the law's injustice," as most criminals designate themselves. "Roger" affected the sincerest contrition for the cowardly aspersion he had cast upon the honour of one of the lady witnesses against him, expressing himself, if I remember rightly, as having been betrayed into the brutal statement "by the maze into which he had been thrown while undergoing cross-examination by Attorney-General Coleridge, who had laid such a trap for him in order to damage his case should he succeed in dragging him into it." He insisted, also, that the Jesuits had been instrumental in effecting his ruin, so as to have the bringing up of "his nephew" and the control of his property in their hands. What his demeanour has been since his removal from Dartmoor to Portsmouth prison is, of course, unknown to me; but if it has been in keeping with what fell under my observation during a couple of years in which he was imprisoned in the former place, he is not likely to emerge from penal servitude as a convert to the Castro-Orton theory of his enemies, or be deterred by the terrible penalty which he has undergone from asserting his claim to the name and property of Sir Roger Tichborne.

LECTURE IX

BOGUS NOBLEMEN (*continued*).

The Aristocratic Impostor—His Qualifications—How the Oracle
is Worked—Exploits of "M le Duc de Montmethuseil,"
Relative of the House of Bourbon-Orleans.

THE bogus nobleman is always of good address, and
shines particularly in conversation, as, I suppose, the
real article does when met with in society. He affects
to treat everybody, save warders, with a lofty disdain
becoming his rank, while the attitude he assumes
when compelled to wheel a barrow, use a shovel, or
carry a slop-can, would remind one of Lord Dundreary
employed in nursing the baby when apprehensive of a
catastrophe. His customary talk is of high living, good
society, university training, foreign travel, horses, wine,
and women; invariably winding up with a resolve to
leave England for ever when released, and reside
abroad for the remainder of life in the enjoyment of
juster laws, sunnier climes, and *recherché* pleasures.
If he can avoid it, the prison nobleman will never

exercise or hold any converse with an avowed pickpocket, and if compelled by accidental association to
do so, he will endeavour to look as indignant and to
assume as much *hauteur* as is consistent with personal
safety: the professional "hooks" being ever ready to
"punch the nose" of their aristocratic associate, or to
designate him as "a blooming swine," in case he should
venture open annoyance or insult. They partake in a
great measure of the characteristics of the begging-
letter writers, already described, but carry their
swindling schemes with a higher hand, and a more
polished finish of execution. Respectable country
hotels, the rural squirearchy, and families of rich manu
facturers or of retired business men constitute the
particular prey of the magsman nobility. The weakness of English national character for titled or distinguished personages is thoroughly understood by the
criminal *noblesse*, and wherever moneyed people are to
be found who are not of the upper ten themselves, but
who dearly love a lord, a baronet, a general, or colonel,
there is the opening for a sham foreign duke, count, or
baron, or native professional aristocrat to introduce
himself to gratify the yearnings of the aspiring circle,
the longings of title-seeking parents having marriageable
daughters, and the vanity of the gossips of the locality,
with the sight, conversation, and familiarity of one of
the class of superior mortals

They usually work in couples, one only appearing upon the scene at a time, the other being employed, at a distance, in the task of aiding his confederate in supporting the *rôle* he has to play. Their qualification for this particular kind of swindle consists, generally, in having at some period of their lives followed either the occupation of a walking gentleman in some travelling theatre, the calling of footman or valet in some gentleman's service, or other occupation in which polite manners and a taste for gentlemanly attire might be acquired. With, of course, special qualifications in addition to some training like the foregoing, and equipped with paste jewellery, and "aristocratic address," the paste nobleman, general, &c, is fully rigged for his professional career.

Their plans and schemes are, of course, shaped more by favouring circumstances than by any fixed mode of procedure. A stranger will arrive, say, at some out-of-the-way country hotel, with a portmanteau or valise, bearing evidence of foreign travel in sundry labels, &c., and marked General or Colonel Somebody, or a Sir, Lord, or other title, and will commence to make inquiries as to shooting, fishing, or other sports of the district, the names of the local gentry, and the salubrious character of the climate thereabouts. If any substantial mansion should chance to be empty in or near the district, he will take mine host into his

THE BOGUS NOBLEMAN'S PLANS

confidence and discuss the suitability of the locality as a
summer, autumn, or winter resort for himself and family
In a day or two letters and society journals will arrive
at the hotel from the confederate addressed to Sir Roland,
Lord Athelstone, or Colonel Montmorency, as the case
may be; and the fact of that part of England or Scotland
being honoured with the presence of a distinguished
individual will immediately spread throughout the
neighbourhood. Instead of thrusting himself upon the
hospitality of some retired grocer or ironmonger with
plenty of money, or other susceptible wealthy individual,
the chances are ten to one that a spirit of rivalry will
exhibit itself among his dupes as to who shall have the
honour of running "the big nob" while sojourning in
their midst. In whatever house he might stay for a
few days, the letters and papers already referred to
would be sure to arrive, and lend their indispensable
aid in sustaining the assumed character of the distinguished or noble stranger. A particular letter, or
perhaps telegram, would contain some vexatious news
from his lawyer or agent, in reference to an unexpected
delay in obtaining rent, quarterly dividends, &c., but
promising a certain remittance in the course of a
week or ten days. In this perplexity the stranger
is reluctantly compelled to trouble some of his new
acquaintances, &c., the farce ending in the usual
manner by the distinguished visitor quite suddenly

disappearing, and allowing the society which had delighted in his company, and had been enraptured with his blue-blood accomplishments, to relapse into its normal repose

I well remember the *furore* of genteel excitement which reigned among the cotton and shoddy aristocracy of the valley of Rossendale, Lancashire, for a few weeks in '68, as the result of the unexpected arrival in its midst of a duke, who was reputed a near relative of the royal house of Bourbon-Orleans. The lucky circumstance which directed his grace's noble footsteps towards that hitherto neglected portion of England, occurred as follows : Captain M——, of the cotton-manufacturing firm of M—— Brothers, and local volunteer military fame, having some business in London in the above year, strolled one day into St. James's Park to take the air, and observing a crowd apparently jostling a gentlemanly-looking person, went to the rescue of the individual, and extricated him from the annoyance to which he appeared to be subjected. The stranger was, as in duty bound, profuse in his thanks to the gallant captain, and requested the favour of knowing to whom he was so much indebted. Cards were immediately exchanged, and upon the captain glancing at the one which was handed him by the stranger, he read thereon—

"M. LE DUC DE MONTMETHUSEIL."

An invitation to honour him with his company at
dinner at his hotel was tendered by the captain, which
was at once most graciously accepted by Monsieur le
Duc Another favour was humbly begged as a consequence of the condescending manner in which the first
was granted, and to the delight of the captain the near
relative of Bourbon royalty consented to accompany his
gallant friend down to the forest of Rossendale, there to
partake of the hospitality so eagerly pressed upon him.
The whole district, from the town of Bacup at the head
of the valley, down to Haslingden near the entrance
thereto (where I resided at the time), was thrown into
a fever of curiosity and excitement in consequence of
the distinction conferred upon its gentry by the presence of a live duke ; and Captain M—— became the
second lion of the district for having been the means of
introducing the noble foreigner to its society. Parties
followed parties in honour of the duke among the
circle in which the captain moved; invitations being
rather selfishly confined to the local Conservatives,
owing to the captain enjoying the position of a recognised leader of that party in and around Bacup; and
the Liberal cotton upper ten of the locality were,
therefore, excluded from making the acquaintance of
the head of the house of Montmethuseil. Stories of
the duke's astonishing condescension began to circulate
among the whole population of Rossendale, and his

person, remarks, and every-day doings became the subject of comment and gossip in every factory in that busy manufacturing valley.

He gratified the desire of the members of the local Volunteer corps, of which his host was captain, by becoming an honorary member, and further exhibited his ducal politeness by dining with the men upon the occasion of a grand military dinner, given by the captain to celebrate the red-letter-day event in the history of the corps. At the ball which followed the duke distinguished himself by his dancing, leading off the dance with the rustic belle of the occasion in a manner that would reflect credit upon the most gallant noble of the Court of his ancestor Louis Quatorze He next granted the diffident request of another local manufacturer, and became godfather to his son, who had fortunately come into the world just in time to receive this ever-to-be-afterwards remembered distinction. Several return invitations were given by the duke to visit his château in Normandy in the following autumn, where, he hoped, his friends from Rossendale would enjoy the excellent shooting that was to be had in that delightful portion of la belle France

Rumour had it that the duke was given the use of his host's cheque-book, pending the arrival of the regular monthly remittance from his Paris bankers, and that, as became a personage of his rank and enormous possessions, he was of a most generous disposition, and possessed of refined and expensive tastes. As it is not according to the customary nature of things, or rules of society, that dukes should spend all their time with cotton manufacturers, no matter how obliging and agreeable, it happened that Monsieur le Duc was summoned away one day by news of an urgent business nature, to the great regret of all who had been honoured by his company and familiarity since his advent to their circle. With his previous invitations reiterated, and a promise to make some provision for his godson, the duke departed—not to be no more heard of, unfortunately for his Rossendale entertainers, but to soon figure in quite another character. Ugly rumours of imposture began soon to circulate, along with calculations as to what "the duke's" patronage must have cost Captain M——, and what the amount of the sums borrowed from other obliging friends; until finally the whole Liberal section of the political world of Rossendale—the leading personages amongst which "the duke" was made to ignore while in the district —was thrown into the greatest transports upon reading in the Manchester papers of a case of bankruptcy in which "M le Duc de Montmethuseil, representing the house of Bourbon," figured along with his father, both of whom had failed in *a tailoring business in that city*, which had been carried on in the name of "C——n and Son." The storm of ridicule which fell on the captain's head, and which had to be borne by his party, kept the whole district in amusement for months after the awful *exposé*; and during the election contest in North-East Lancashire, which followed the dissolution of Parliament in 1868, the Tories in Rossendale district lost the services of Captain M——, as it was impossible for him to appear in public without hearing himself shouted after as "Duke, Duke!" He, however, made a clean breast of the whole affair in a letter to one of the local papers, and accepted the entire blame attaching to the introduction of the "duke" into the society of the locality; merely adding, as a kind of return fire to the fun-poking artillery of his Liberal opponents, that the "duke," while in London, had taken in some prominent members of the Liberal party

Although thirteen years have gone by since the foregoing swindle was perpetrated, its memory is still alive in Rossendale, and will live as long as party strife delights in exposing the weakness or ridiculous occurrences in the character or history of political adversaries

LECTURE X.

CLASS III. MAGSMEN (*continued*).

Aristocratic Impostures (*continued*)—Their Select Party in Dartmoor—Adventures of Bertrand Ashley, *alias* Count von Ostrogg, von Sobriski, &c.

DARTMOOR contained several of this class of impostor during the first three years of my time in that prison. Most of them had succeeded in obtaining admission to the stocking-knitting party, which, in consequence, became known among the rest of the prisoners as "the upper-ten push." This branch of convict work, employing from a dozen to twenty prisoners, was carried on under a large shed in one of the prison yards, in conjunction with another class of light labour, namely, stone-breaking; and as this latter more democratic employment was that at which I was employed for a time, I was in a position where I could observe the conduct of the "nobility," and note such traits of their character, tone of conversation, and general demeanour as the circumstances of the situation might call into play.

The stocking party numbered among its members a Russian "count," an English "major-general," a colonel, a "captain," the "heir-apparent to an earldom" already alluded to, and other distinguished individuals claiming somewhat less exalted positions in the world of importance and fame. The colonel was the only *bona fide* aristocrat in the crowd. He had been at one period of his life the governor of an island under the British Crown, and owed his imprisonment to some offence or other the nature of which I could never rightly learn. He was an exceedingly polite and genial sort of person, and merits no further comment in connection with the impostors who formed his labour associates.

Nothing could be more laughter-provoking to any one capable of finding food for amusement in the eccentricities of human character than the studied deportment and conversation of these exquisite shams. A company of old maids emulous to appear younger than appearances would warrant could not exhibit more ridiculous expressions of face or of carriage than were presented by this assortment of precious rascals in their efforts to equal or outdo the colonel in the manner of bearing which sat quite natural upon his whole personal conduct. If one could only "wreak his feelings upon expression" while observing and listening to that select society, it would be an easy matter to set in motion the risible propensity of the most austere physiognomy. The heir-apparent to the British Crown was simply "Wales," in the "I-know-the-prince-well-you-know" style of speech affected by the "heir apparent" to the bogus earldom, while the "major-general" adopted a corresponding familiarity of expression in all matters relating to the military ranks, from the Duke of Cambridge down to sarcastic commentaries upon Volunteer sham fights.

The Russian "count," however, was the personage who claimed most of my attention, not particularly on account of his distinguished rank, but from the fact that he was really of Russian birth, though imprisoned under the name of "Bertrand Victor A——" As he presents a fair sample of the "foreign-nobleman" class of impostor, already partly sketched in the episode of M. le Duc de Montmethuseil, I will finish my description of this type of criminal with a brief account of Bertrand Victor, and some of his subsequent adventures He was a man of about thirty-five years of age, close upon six feet in height, and of very good address, the features presenting very slight traces of his Slavonic origin; while his manners, like those of most foreigners, were gentlemanly and agreeable,

VOL. I.   H

particularly when he was desirous of making a good
impression   His introduction to me was brought about
by the fact that "the upper-ten" stocking party and
that in which I was employed exercised together for
half an hour each evening after labour; and as talking
was permitted (at that time) while prisoners were
exercising, there was ample opportunity for listening
to adventures, and forming opinions of the prisoners
with whom I was thus brought into contact.   In my
first chat with Bertrand Victor I learned that he was the
son of a distinguished Russian; that he had been sent
to England to complete his education; had studied for
some time at Oxford University : had afterwards joined
the English navy as surgeon, and had managed, somehow
or other, not explained, to find himself at that period
(1872) within two years of completing a sentence of
seven in penal servitude   His English prison name
was, of course, an assumed one, and his family were
kept in complete ignorance of his being an inmate
of an English convict establishment

He had made a tour of Europe, saving a visit to
Ireland; and, as he would be in possession of a fair
fortune when again at liberty, and would be most
anxious to withdraw from English society for a year
or so after liberation, he was thinking of selecting that
interesting country for a twelve months' sojourn when
restored to freedom.   "Where would he be likely to

meet with polite and intellectual society out of Dublin;
he having heard that that was principally an English
peopled city?" My reply being neither satisfactory
nor complimentary to this proffer of distinguished
patronage of Ireland, Bertrand Victor was suddenly
reminded, from conversations he had had with other
Fenian prisoners while in Portland Prison, that the
Irish must be intellectually inferior to the English,
exceptions existing, of course, in Irishmen who had
won imperishable fame in the walks of English
literature, &c. This is a summary of our conversation,
or rather, of his talk to me on the occasion of our first
introduction His command of languages was really
marvellous, amply sustaining the well-known linguistic
fame of his countrymen His English was next to
faultless in pronunciation, and he could converse with
equal facility in French, German, and Italian, while
he had also a reputed knowledge of Danish, Swedish,
and Polish, with, of course, the perfect use of the
Russian In addition, he was as well read in English
literature, and as well versed in the etiquette of
English society, as an ordinary college-educated Englishman He was, on the whole, about the most
singular and the most accomplished individual with
whom I conversed during my imprisonment in Dartmoor. In 1873 he was transferred from that prison to
Chatham along with a batch of other convicts, from

which place he was discharged in the beginning of the following year, his whole sentence of seven years having then expired

Early in the summer of 1874 a student of E—— College engaged as foreign tutor one Count Sobriski, a Polish nobleman, who, like many more of his countrymen, had been exiled on account of his efforts to free that ill-fated land from Russian vassalage. His extraordinary linguistic accomplishments, engaging address, and distinguished birth, rendered the count an important addition to the social circle round E—— College Among the families to which the count had obtained an introduction, through his pupil, was one which consisted of a wealthy gentleman and only daughter, the latter the heiress of her father's posses- sions The lady's beauty fascinated the gallant count from the first sight of her lovely person, while the *distingué* bearing, wonderful conversational abilities, and, above all, the noble rank of the exiled Pole, made no less an agreeable impression upon the susceptibilities of the lady's heart. This mutual appreciation soon begat a declaration of love from the count, which proved both acceptable to the fair one and agreeable to papa, who was, naturally enough, pleased at the prospect of having his daughter so married that she could figure as a countess in the ranks of society The count was, therefore, the recognised lover of the heiress.

After a wooing as short as it was successful, the count, as was pardonable under the circumstances, was most eager to crown his happiness with the right of a husband. Like all love-smitten adorers, he pressed for an early marriage-day, and had his prayer granted in the appointment of an approximate date upon which to lead the bride to the altar. But, alas! how oft has cruel accident marred the plans of Hymen, and thwarted the love aspirations of enamoured swain and languishing beauty! Why, when the course of true affection *does* run smooth, will the tyrant of romantic love appear on the scene, in some form or other, and snap in twain the flowery links that are to bind two hearts for ever?

The young lady became unwell. The doctor prescribed Margate for a fortnight, and the count was pressed to accompany his darling and her papa to that (unfortunately for the count) largely frequented resort. The day after the arrival of the party the lovers were strolling along the beach, the count in all likelihood adopting the words of Claude Melnotte, and picturing to the raptured fancy of his Pauline some romantic castle by the waters of a Polish Como, where they would dwell in conjugal happiness, and laugh to scorn the impotency of descriptive genius to paint in poetic words a love like theirs, when—Good gracious! What has happened? The count has stopped, as if struck with a bullet, declares, watch in hand, that an appointment of a most vital family nature *must* be kept in London that very afternoon, and thereupon dashes off to the railway station like a shot.

A few moments after, when the young lady and her papa were recovering somewhat from the surprise into which the count's singular behaviour had thrown them, two men who had been following the movements of the party on the beach approached, and, after saluting the lady, informed them that the individual whom they had just seen in the company of the gentleman and his daughter was a recently-released convict and most accomplished impostor! Some swooning followed, of course, the fainting lady was driven to an hotel, a doctor was summoned, and thus ended the dream of the would-be countess, and with her and her ambitious papa my story has nothing further to do. But to follow the flight of the amorous Sobriski During the count's sojourn in E—— it transpired that certain property in jewellery, money, and plate belonging to his pupil and the latter's friends became missing, some of which was discovered in the count's apartments during his love trip to Margate It was for this he was "wanted" by the emissaries of the law. After his escape from Margate he was traced to a west-end lodging-house, was surprised, but not captured, in the middle of the night, and had to make his way over the roof in anything but full dress   He succeeded in eluding the efforts of his pursuers for some weeks after this narrow escape, but finally succumbed to a stratagem on the part of the detectives who were at the time acquainted with the locality where he was in hiding.   A paragraph was made to appear in a London daily, containing, as a piece of apparently authentic intelligence, the informa· tion of Count Sobriski's having baffled the vigilance of Scotland Yard, and succeeded in making his escape to Belgium.   Thrown off his guard upon reading this paragraph, and believing his pursuers to have followed a wrong scent, the count emerged from his hiding-place and took himself to Burton-on-Trent, there to engage in any enterprise which fortune might kindly place in his way.   There was but time for the intelligence to spread in the neighbourhood of his hotel that a Swedish nobleman of great accomplishments and fortune, one Count von Ostrogg, was staying there, before the London detectives appeared on the scene, captured their man, and terminated his swindling career for the second time in England. His trial disclosed most of the foregoing and other facts concerning successful frauds since being liberated from Chatham some six or eight months previously, and the judge awarded the unfortunate " count " a sentence of fifteen years' penal servitude.   Among the many " old familiar faces " that met my view upon attending

service in the Catholic chapel in this prison the first
Sunday of my arrival here in February last, was that of
" Bertrand Victor A——," *alias* " Count Sobriski," a
convict this time in the name of von Ostrogg. I was
informed by a French thief while in Dartmoor that the
" Russian," as he was familiarly termed, had completed
two terms of imprisonment on the continent before
coming to England—one in the prison of Konigsberg,
and the other in Moulins, near Paris.

Allowing five years for both of these terms, in the
absence of the correct sentences, the " count," upon the
termination of his present " lagging," will have undergone seven-and-twenty years of imprisonment — a
terrible penalty, in all faith, to pay for the life of an
accomplished rogue, offering very little inducement
to mortals who aspire to be considered of noble birth
and station to leave the paths of honest labour, and
the safer, if less sensational, position of ordinary
citizenship.

The remaining types of criminal belonging to the
order of magsmen do not call for any specific description—such as medical quacks, and other mock professors who are seldom introduced into convict society,
being more acquainted with county prisons and city
bridewells in short sentences of one or two years.

The magsman is the most intellectual of society's
professional criminals, and not the least singular feature

in the character of these swindlers is the possession, by a very large portion of them, of unusual talents, great fertility of resource, and thorough knowledge both of human nature and of the world, which, if but joined to an observance of moral precept in some business or professional pursuit, would enable them to fulfil a share of the functions of social life with success to themselves and no small benefit to civilised society It is a deplorable fact, but nevertheless true, that not two per cent. of this class ever abandon their dishonest pursuits until the diseases contracted in the indulgence of immoral habits, and the wear and tear of penal servitude, commit them, in comparatively early life, to the custody of the grim jailer Death, never more to prey upon the property or play upon the weakness of their species.

LECTURE XI

CLASS III.   SECTION 2.   "HOOKS."

General Characteristics — Difference between Hooks and "Snatchers" — Influences which Nourish the Pickpocket Class—Professional Pride—The Cadger-Thief Repudiated—"The Man of the World"—His Accomplishments—Lady Hooks—How they Work—The Scientific Method of Pocket-picking—The various Dodges of the Hook.

HOOKS.—These individuals, who are also known as "gunns" and "buzzers," in prison slang, constitute the pickpocket class in its various specialties. They can be subdivided into three orders · "men of the world," or professional hooks; ordinary "snatchers," or young and inexperienced thieves; and "thief-cadgers," the lowest species of the class   While distinct in their manner of thieving, these three sections of the great pickpocket order, excepting to some extent, the first, have their "professional calling" so well outlined in gait, constant use of slang, furtive looks, almost total want of tact in their ordinary conduct, with an instinctively suspicious manner in almost all their actions, that they are as easily distinguishable from the other criminals of a prison as they are recognisable to their constant pursuers, the police, when abroad in the world. Nineteen out of every twenty of this whole order will have served one or more terms of imprisonment in county jails previous to an *entrée* into penal servitude; while thirty per cent. will be re-convicted convicts, having a "lagging" or two scored against them in penal records They are among the most troublesome men in a prison, and will steal anything upon which they can lay their fingers, from another prisoner's bread to any article belonging to the place which can be taken in spite of warders' vigilance. They can no more resist the temptation to lay hands upon anything of value that may chance to lie in their way, than can a cat forbear to seize a mouse which runs across its path. Thieving with these unfortunate beings seems to be a kind of instinct, the incessant promptings of which is beyond the power of their stunted mental and moral faculties to withstand, and the complete subduing or even temporary subjection of whose workings neither punishment nor kindness, teaching nor threatening, can in the least degree effect. Give one of them three days' bread-and-water diet for going into another prisoner's cell and stealing his bread, and he will commit a similar theft

the hour after the termination of that punishment, if
he thinks he has a chance of not being caught in the
act.   Throw a tempting lady's pocket, or a carelessly
hanging watch-chain in the way of a " hook " the week
following his liberation from a seven years' imprisonment, and he will forget everything he has suffered, and
all that may happen again, in an effort to possess himself
of what appeals to this predominant instinct of his perverted being.   The removing of an habitual pickpocket
from among the public by a sentence of penal servitude
under the existing system is simply deterring him for
that period from troubling society, and will have as
much effect upon his conduct when he finds his way
into the world again as the pruning of a garden shrub
would have upon its growth.

Of all the social desperadoes that belong to the present civilised order of things, this class is, *par excellence*,
society's special contribution to its own punishment.
Bred in the slums of London, Manchester, Liverpool,
Glasgow, Birmingham, Dublin, or other large city, of
low, and invariably drunken parents, often the offspring
of unfortunate women; sent out thieving when but eight
or nine years old by mothers who are little better than
prostitutes; what wonder that these wretched creatures
should grow up as ignorant of right and as prone to
snatch at whatever comes within their reach as the less
depraved, irrational animals, which but follow a law of

their nature in seizing upon anything that excites their craving? Would society rid itself of this social pest, or rather, would it emasculate the agencies which nourish the infancy and train the maturity of this particular class of criminal, let the offspring of crime and pauperism be taken as young as possible from the atmosphere of vice or degrading squalor in which they are to be found, and be removed to kindergarten schools, entirely away from parents who will only rear them for a similar pursuit to their own. Let the State demolish what remains of city slums. Let every low drink-house be swept away, and let society apply itself in solemn earnest to provide not only better houses for the poor but opportunities for more elevating recreation, and then, and not till then, will the low pickpocket and the bruiser type of ruffian begin to be improved off the face of civilised life.

Taking the pickpocket class in the order in which I have arranged its several sections, the "man of the world" comes up for first description. He is the professional or skilled rifler of other people's pockets, and differs in many respects from his less experienced, and of course less exalted, brethren, the common "snatcher" and the "cadger." Of the latter he holds the smallest possible opinion, and, like the "honourable thief" of the burglar class, looks upon him as a disgrace to the accomplished order of theft, and seldom associates with him when out of prison. I one day received some abusive language from one of this most despised class of criminal, and I excited the curiosity of a "hook" in the party as to why I did not "hit the blooming cadger a punch on the nose"? My reply being that I could take no offence at anything a thief might say, the hook promptly corrected me by exclaiming, "You think *him* a *thief*? He never was anything of the sort in his blooming life. He is a blooming *cadger!*" Had I called a Dublin policeman a Senior Fellow of Trinity College within the hearing of one of its students, my statement could not have been more emphatically or indignantly repudiated.

The "man of the world," as he loves to style himself, is so called, not from any resemblance to the similarly designated personage of polite society, but from the fact of his accomplishment being such that he can follow his profession anywhere—in the streets, riding in 'busses or railway trains, or wherever in London or the provinces inclination or business may direct his course He is generally "an old hand," that is, over twenty-five years of age, and a confirmed jailbird He will turn his talents to any other job in the way of thieving that may turn up in his travels "around the world," from robbing a hen-roost in a country place to an attempt at burglary where he believes there are no city policemen to spoil his game.

In London and other large cities he is generally in
Co. with a "lady hook," or a "pal" of his own sex
and particular walk.

The lady, as is usually the case when criminally
educated or inclined, is the cleverer artist in the
calling she pursues, and is very often the only active
worker of such a partnership, especially when working along with a hook who has been three or four
times "lagged" for having allowed himself to be
caught.

The "lady" is always provided with a dress having
long and wide sleeves, within which she can move her
hand and "hooks" (fingers) easily when standing or
sitting close to the individual whose pocket she is
anxious to explore. The gentleman is also provided
either with a similarly furnished coat, or he carries
a light overall, rug, or shawl upon his arm, so as to
disguise as far as possible the working of the operating
member while rifling a pocket. Some pockets are, of
course, more readily got into than others, and all individuals are not good game in this particular branch of
thieving. Hooks, male or female, seldom exercise their
talents upon closely wrapped or wide-awake looking
personages. If a pocket is to be picked in a bus, railway car, or where a number of people are sitting or
standing close together, the theft may be performed by
the hand nearest the party who is to be robbed—the

cloak or other article of dress which will be carelessly thrown over such hand being made to hide what is going on underneath—while the operator is chatting with his prey or otherwise diverting attention from his efforts to obtain purse or money. But the off hand, or that farthest from the side of the victim, is more frequently the extracting medium. Assuming a gentleman to be about having his watch stolen by a clever pickpocket, while standing in a street, or looking into a window, the operation would be performed, other circumstances favouring the thief, as follows. The hook would introduce himself by asking the gentleman's opinion as to the worth of a ring, scarf-pin, or other such article which he, the speaker, had just purchased cheap in the belief that the ring was really gold, or that the pin contained a diamond. The article upon which the gentleman's judgment was to be pronounced would be given to him by that one of the thief's hands which would be next to the person of the gentleman, and which would be carrying the cloak or overall already referred to, while the other hand would be moved horizontally, and from the elbow only, across the thief's breast, and under cover of the cloak or coat, towards the watch-pocket of the victim. The essential point in the performance is to divert the victim's attention as much as possible from the neighbourhood of his watch, and for the performer to speak and act as if the operating hand belonged to a third party, which could be neither seen nor felt by the victim. If the watch is fastened to its chain by a bar, it is deftly broken off ("breaking off a jerry") by the thief's fingers; but if by a swivel, it must either be put back into the owner's pocket, allowed to hang by its chain and so expose the nature of the whole transaction, or be snatched, and the after proceedings made a run on the part of the hook, and a cry of "Stop thief!" on that of the owner of the watch. The necessary introduction to the successful perpetration of the robbery may be effected in a score of other ways besides the one described; such as asking information as to the whereabouts of a certain locality, requesting the favour of having a slip of paper read containing an address or other writing which the stranger cannot read, offering of flowers, books, &c., for sale, and desiring their inspection. In all such instances, however, the thief is certain to be carrying some loose article of dress or convenient parcel upon one arm, without the aid of which it would be well-nigh impossible to "break off a jerry," scientifically or in daylight, without instant detection.

The "lady hook" frequently carries a small pair of very sharp and peculiarly formed shears, with which she very often cuts her way into a stubborn or well-concealed pocket belonging to members of her own sex, while the male artist occasionally employs a lancet-like penknife for the purpose of cutting out the breast-pocket of a buttoned-up coat, which he believes may contain a pocket-book or other property.

This, the clever type of pickpocket, is generally pretty well dressed, is possessed of a fair amount of intelligence, and frequents places of public resort, theatres, churches, races, &c. One who was an admitted adept in this branch of crime, and from whom I have obtained most of my information upon the "art" of thieving, told me that he had taken more than one purse and watch out of the British Museum, "where," he remarked, "it was quite easy to fix the attention of the victim by pointing out the excellencies of a picture or statue with one hand while 'hooking' with the other." He never went to "business" without furnishing himself with the indispensable cloak or wrap for the arm, the use for which I have previously described.

LECTURE XII.

CLASS III. HOOKS (*continued*).

' Chucking a Dummy "—How Places of Worship are occasionally
"Surprised"—"Snatchers" constitute the Youth of a Prison
—How "Brought Out"— Their Places of Resort — The
Pestilent Influence of the Literature of Rascaldom—How
Honest Boys are Made Thieves—The Thief-Cadger—His
Schemes.

I WAS startled while at work one day in Dartmoor by
seeing the hook who was last described leap off the
seat next mine, in a shed where our party was stone-
breaking, as if he had been cast by a giant into the
middle of the place, there fall upon his back, and go
through the most horrible writhings I had ever wit-
nessed. His eyes appeared as if bursting from their
sockets, blood and foam oozed from his mouth, while
four other prisoners could scarcely hold his arms, so
fearfully was his whole body convulsed, forming altogether one of the most sickening sights I ever beheld.
After three or four minutes' apparent agony he quieted

down, and was carried off to the infirmary. Being an exceedingly intelligent young fellow, I could not help expressing to the warder what a pity it was that one so full of life and health should be afflicted with so terrible a malady as fits; whereupon he simply gave me for reply a look which, if capable of being put into action, would bode no good to the back of the prisoner just removed to the hospital as an afflicted wretch apparently deserving of the commiseration of any man possessing the feelings of ordinary humanity. "Yes, it *is* a pity," he answered at last, and strode away, as if leaving unuttered, "that the doctor will not report him to the director for a flogging!"

Only a few days elapsed, after this incident, until I found myself almost of the same opinion. The object of my pity returned to his work after three days' hospital treatment, and I took the first opportunity that offered to fall in file with him at evening exercise, to learn how he became subject to such an affliction. I was thunderstruck at the reply which he made to my inquiry—"I never had a real fit in all my life! What you saw the other day was what we call 'chucking a dummy,' or, as you might name it, in your less expressive manner of speaking, 'counterfeiting a fit.' We sometimes," continued he, "make good use of this dodge when a number of us go to 'do' a chapel, or meeting-place of would-be pious individuals. In the most appropriate part of the proceedings one of us 'chucks a dummy.' There is, of course, an immense sensation created in the audience—women come with their scent-bottles, men rush for water, great sympathy is expressed by others; while the hooks are all the time busy at the pockets of the pitying crowd and easing them of their purses. Half-a-dozen of us have taken upwards of fifty pounds out of a congregation on one Sunday evening by means of this trick."

"But do you not consider you are making it bad for those poor wretches who really are so afflicted by doing that revolting action here?" I ventured to object.

"Well, as to that," he answered, "you might as well plead on behalf of those who lose their purses. I chucked that one the other day in order to get removed from the cell I was then in, which was next to that of a blooming swine whom I did not like; and I had no other excuse with which to go to the infirmary until my cell would be filled by some one else, so that I should be located elsewhere."

He also informed me that the same horrible trick is often performed in the open street, in a public-house, or other such place, where it would be likely to gather a crowd for confederate thieves to operate upon.

After undergoing two or three sentences of penal servitude, the hooks employ, or rather train, young boys in the tricks for which they have been so deservedly punished themselves, and they seldom venture again upon the work of any job that is not deemed perfectly safe of accomplishment. In consequence of this they are about the worst type of criminal against which society has to defend itself. Their reformation is as hopeless as would be the efforts to wash a negro white. They make the most frequent use of slang of all thieves, and have a cipher language by which they can converse with each other without being understood by the uninitiated

Snatchers.—This type of pickpocket bears the same resemblance to his superior brother, the hook, as the apprentice to some trade does to his master in the matter of proficiency. The average age of prisoners of this branch who are found in a convict establishment will not be more than twenty. They constitute the youth of a prison, and their one great ambition is to be thought clever enough to have performed some daring or successful theft after having been " brought out " by some renowned hook. They will almost all be found to have had drunken and semi-prostitute mothers, who will have sent them a-thieving when quite young, and to have undergone some years' confinement in "the school," as they term the reformatory. They are always taken in hand by the old " faikes " (old experienced criminals), trained in all the ways of theft, and fixed for life in a circle of reproductive crime, between careers of thieving and drunkenness, when at liberty, and alternate terms of imprisonment as convicted felons   Numbers of them are also in keeping of prostitutes, by whom they are enticed into or made to follow the thieving profession.   Their most frequent mode of theft is simply to snatch at a watch-chain, and trust to darkness and fleetness of foot for an escape with chain and watch.   They also steal in this manner from ladies any article of value which they observe being carried in a careless manner.   Lord Mayor's Day in London is their grand harvest time, but a harvest time for the detectives in their capture also.   They very often move in gangs, surrounding a man who may be "sporting a red jerry" (a "loud" exhibition of gold guard), and snatch his watch amid the jostling.   They are also very busy at Epsom during race time, and ply their game as well at public gatherings, Hyde Park meetings, street-corner preaching, &c.   Owing to their youth they are more susceptible to the reforming efforts of priest and chaplain than any other section of a prison, country offenders excepted.   Very few, however, are ever permanently rescued from the life with which they were made acquainted when young, owing chiefly to their early training in dishonesty, and from invariably falling again into the hands of old thieves or abandoned women after being discharged from prison.   The frequent re-convictions of these young thieves is, in nineteen cases out of twenty, the immediate consequence of these two most fruitful of all the agencies of criminal pursuit. They are quite as troublesome in prison as the hook, and with him swell the record of extra punishments in the convict establishments. They are generally of a poor physique, being debilitated through the various diseases that result from neglected childhood, unwholesome food, and the venereal scourges so prevalent amongst the criminal classes generally. While possessing a deal of low cunning, together with a moderate intelligence chiefly acquired in reformatories and county prisons, they are the most ignorant of the thieving class, saving the country thieves and cadgers, exhibiting in all matters beyond their vicious pursuits an animal-like stupidity and want of judgment and tact, which place them intellectually lower than even the country thief, who can scarcely read or write.

Among this class of young thieves are often found youths who have had honest parents and a proper bringing up, and who are exceptions to the foregoing remarks on the physical inferiority and ignorance of the generality of snatchers. These are the victims of such works as *Blueskin, Three-finger Jack, Jack Sheppard, Claud Duval, Dick Turpin,* and the various other pestiferous criminal novelettes which have obtained such an immense circulation among boys of the industrial

classes of these countries during the past twenty years
The writers of these thief-making sheets represent their
pickpocket, burglar, or highwayman hero in pictur-
esque colours, and surround their adventures, in attacks
on police and robbery of victims, with such descriptions
of daring exploits, stirring incidents, hair-breadth escapes,
and gallantry towards the fair sex, that the real immediate nature of their pursuits becomes divested of
its inherent wrong, and presents to the young and
inexperienced mind nothing but a course of romantic
adventure, to emulate which is more chivalrous than
censurable, and to surpass in daring but the high-road
to boyish conception of fame   Hundreds of bright
intelligent boys have been torn from the homes of
respectable parents through the instrumentality of this
literature of rascaldom, and have become cast, in most
cases, for their whole future among the felon ranks of
habitual criminal life.   Others, of a similar honest
rearing, have fallen into habits of crime from association with abandoned women, by whom they are sent
upon thieving errands, "in order to show their pluck
and the stuff they are made of," but in reality to
obtain money or anything else that will provide these
wretched beings with drink and pleasure

Thief-Cadgers—This, the pariah order of habitual
criminal, is designated "the cadger" from uniting two
callings in his mode of thieving—begging (cadging)

and " shop-lifting " They usually assume the poverty-stricken or hard-up looks of the common mendicant, and ply their real pursuit under cover of a disguise that is calculated to arouse pity for their seemingly wretched lot, rather than suspicion of their intentions. Mostly all the theft known as shop-lifting (stealing articles exhibited for sale in or around shops), so frequently committed in large cities, is performed by this type of thief   He will beg from house to house in town or country, and "bone" anything of value which he may find unwatched or otherwise unprotected in his way   If he finds a house at which he calls for alms empty—that is, if the owners or persons in charge are absent for a short time, or employed in another part of the house—the thief-cadger will help himself to whatever is worth "boning" and of easy removal, and is off and away with limb as nimble and eye as quick as these organs were probably made to appear the reverse a few minutes previously. They also, in London particularly, lie in wait for children running errands, and rob them of whatever they may be carrying at the time. When on the thieving path, both in cities and large towns, they provide themselves with slips of paper containing an address, which, if surprised in a house or shop ere commencing to steal, they will produce, and ask whoever chances to appear on the scene to be so kind as to read it for them, as they (the cadgers) are

no "scholards." "Set a thief to catch a thief" is
referable to this order, as they are generally the
informers of their own class, and are, as a rule, the
means of betraying to the police the successful workers
of a burglary or other job performed by their more
skilful brethren in crime. In prison they are always
ready to "put away" (inform upon) any other prisoner
who may have anything contraband on his person or in
his cell. In consequence of these qualities they are
treated by almost all prisoners with contempt, and are
often savagely beaten by other convicts, who look upon
them as instruments in the hands of the warders for
spying upon other prisoners They are about the
lowest and most repulsive species of human being to
be met with anywhere. They spend most of their
miserable lives in prison, where they enjoy a better
scale of living than falls to their lot outside. When
living for a short time in liberty, that is, between two
sentences, they sleep in out-houses, the parks, cabs,
under arches, and other such places. Their prowling in
the guise of beggars subjects the real mendicant, the
broken-down workman or victim of misfortune who
dreads the stigma of workhouse pauperism, to unjust
and unmerited suspicion, which often makes it difficult
for these poor creatures to obtain a crust outside of
the institution which they dread to enter.

LECTURE XIII.

CLASS IV.

The "BRUISER" His Photo.—What other Criminals think of him—His Accomplishments—How he Works his Game— His Attacks on Warders

The ' BOUNCE": The "Injured Husband" Trick—The Lady Accomplice—The Class from which Victims are Selected— How the Black-mail is Levied—Extent to which this Game is carried on.

The "COMMON BOUNCE": Infamous Nature of this Crime.

THE *Bruiser*—This, the fourth and last class into which I have divided the inmates of a convict prison, is the least numerous of the four, but, as if in recompense for that, is the most dangerous of them all   I have already observed that the bruiser is the nearest approach to Dickens's hero Bill Sykes, so far as the criminal in the flesh can well correspond to that of the novelist. Murderers are never, however, found in this class in prison. This is opposed to the popular opinion, which believes that classification of offence more or less defines classification of prison conduct also. But I

have shown in my remarks upon Class I that the
convicts who have imbrued their hands in the blood of
their fellow-men are among the most docile prisoners
and the most amenable to prison discipline Neither
does the bruiser class necessarily include all those who
rob with violence, though numbers of that desperate
order are of course found in its ranks

The bruiser is a peculiar and composite criminal,
made up of the meanness and non-professional traits of
a cadger and the pretensions of a pugilist, together
with the cowardice of a street-corner bully joined to
all the reputed accomplishments of Bill Sykes, saving
that gentleman's proneness to commit murder. He is
as clumsy at the commission of a theft as would be a
ploughman in the repairing of a watch, and is never
credited by the other thieves with the possession of
either smartness, ability, fame, or "honour." He is
the very embodiment of idleness inside of prison as he
doubtless is outside, and to this fact, together with the
thoroughly communistic regulation of the convict com-
monwealth, that those who will not work must pay for
their laziness in the matter of diet, is due the greater
portion of the bruiser's violence in prison, for which
he receives additional and merited punishment. His
prison talk is generally of all the people he has
"slugged" (beaten), from "coppers" (policemen) to
reputed pugilists, or men otherwise renowned for their

fistic prowess. He is, in consequence of this talk,
spoken of derisively by his prison companions as " a
bloke who has a private churchyard of his own outside
where he buries all whose lights he puts out." He
will not unfrequently " turn over " another thief—
that is, rob a pickpocket or other such artist of the
" swag," which the latter may have " boned " by his
skill. His chief support, however, is his " old woman,"
as he always terms the unfortunate creature who cohabits with him, and whom he frequently ill-uses in the
most brutal and cowardly manner; and in addition to
compelling her to procure him money in the ordinary
manner in which such creatures earn it, he very often
resorts to a method which bears some resemblance
to the crimes next to be described, namely " carrying
the kosh " (bludgeon). Armed with this weapon,
which he carries in his sleeve, he keeps in sight of
his " old woman " for " protection," and upon any one
engaging the latter in conversation in the parks or
unfrequented places, rushes to the rescue of his " wife
or sister," and offers the person thus caught the alter-
native of being punched into mince-meat in no time,
or the forking out of all the loose cash he may have
upon his person   As the latter demand is not generally
very pleasing to the character of men on whom the
attempts are made, desperate fights are of frequent
occurrence, in which the policeman occasionally figures

when, in consequence, the offence becomes known as robbery with violence. He will never represent himself as having been "lagged" for anything else but "slugging a copper"—a deed always highly applauded in convict society, and for very obvious reasons On the whole the bruiser is the most brutal and criminal-like in appearance of all convicts, and takes rank with the lowest of those already described in ignorance, and all the repulsive features of avowed and unconscionable crime. His attacks upon prison warders are more frequently prompted by a repugnance to labour than from any innate love of thrashing somebody. An offence of this kind is put back by the governor for the adjudication of the visiting director, who comes to a convict prison for such among other purposes once every month or six weeks, and until the offender is thus dealt with he is confined in a separate cell and exempt from labour It is but the most stupid of lazy brutes who would act in this manner, as an attack upon a warder is always met by a defence in which the bruiser receives more than he bargains for, together with the additional punishment of the cat, which is awarded him by the visiting director. To finish the picture of this ugly jail-bird, I have been informed that numbers of his class go through the performance already described, employing their sisters as the necessary female confederate.

The Bouncer.—The class of crime represented by
this, the slang name of its professors, seldom or never
figures in a criminal prosecution, although it is of
the commonest occurrence in most large cities, especially in London, and is the means of extracting
large sums of money from many gentlemen in
society who would be proof against any other species
of robbery or fraud   It is very difficult to describe
what it exactly means, or the agencies employed in
entrapping its victims, but I will endeavour to give
an outline of it as far as decency of expression will
permit.   It is divided into two branches—"the injured
husband" and "the common bouncer."   In carrying
out the robbery by the former trick, "a lady"
is indispensable, and she is. of course, either of the
class of unfortunates, or one of the very numerous
women who cohabit with professional thieves, and who
pursue thieving likewise, but who are not of the
ordinary abandoned following.   Her male confederate is sure to be an old jail-bird, or thief-trainer,
who has fallen back upon this class of crime after
having served two or three sentences of penal servitude ; for the reason that the police seldom catch, and
victims dare not prosecute, those who perpetrate it
The manner of working the "injured husband" dodge
is as follows.   The lady, provided with a moderate
share of good looks, and well dressed, lies in wait for

some elderly, well-to-do gentleman who has been previously fixed upon as a victim by her "husband" (the-jail bird in question), or occasionally one who may not have been thus selected; and by arts known to that class of women induce the victim to accompany her to her home or lodgings, she invariably representing herself as being a servant or seamstress out of employment, and of respectable character. If the ruse succeeds, the victim is decoyed to some place known for this class of crime alone, and not to an ordinary brothel, and is closely and secretly followed by the vigilant "husband." No sooner has the victim found himself *tête-a-tête* with his betrayer, than the door is burst open, and in rushes the "husband" in the wildest state of excitement, brandishing either a knife, bludgeon, or pistol, and shouting that he has seen his wife enter that house with another man, and declaring that he will take her life or that of her paramour The "fix" of the victim can be better imagined than described. The wife falls on her knees before the infuriated "husband" and goes through the performance of endeavouring to soften his resentment against the victim, but is, of course, spurned by her wronged and virtuous spouse. Finally the "husband" summons the owner of the house and demands the presence of a policeman, in order that he may have justice at the hands of the law, and secure the exposure of the old

scoundrel who has ruined his happiness for life, and
covered his honest name with disgrace, &c., &c. This
threat of exposure and the acting by which it is accompanied, has the desired effect upon the victim, who, of
course, would part probably with half his wealth rather
than his family, his friends, or the public should believe
him capable of such conduct. The weeping "false
one" is removed from the apartment and a bargain
struck between the somewhat appeased "husband"
and the "betrayer"—seldom less than a loss of all the
money in the immediate possession of the entrapped
party, with a written promise of more if he be known
to be a man of wealth and position. The game seldom
ends with the capture thus described, especially if the
victim is prominently known in the locality or in society.
A system of black-mailing is carried on, perhaps for
years after, by which the individual who has allowed
himself to fall into such a snare is compelled, under
threats of public exposure, or a visit to his wife and
family, to pay hundreds of pounds. Scores of such
victims are moving about in society at the present hour
with this penalty held over them by some successful
bouncer or other, for having been guilty of a momentary
indiscretion   One who had repeatedly acted the part
of an "injured husband," and who was for a time in
a party in which I was employed in Dartmoor, has
supplied me with the foregoing particulars of this trick,

which he called "playing upon the vices of rich old
rascals" I was further assured by him, that he, on
one occasion, compelled one of his victims to procure
him an invitation to a Mansion House banquet under a
threat of the above kind. He further gave me the
name of a once prominent M.P, now dead, who had
been successfully black-mailed by himself and his "gal"
during a period of five years, for having once succumbed
to this dodge. Whether this after-shadowing of a
person who has been fooled in this way be considered
a merited retribution for his folly or not, is beside the
question; but the number of aged and highly respectable men in wealthy and professional circles who are
under this punishment, in London alone, would astonish
society if it could be accurately ascertained. It would,
of course, be ridiculous to dream of putting men on
their guard against this species of robbery, as no one in
his senses would admit himself capable of being betrayed
into such a position; but the exhibition of a little
moral courage on the part of the victim would not
unfrequently put an end to the black-mailing which
the appearance of moral cowardice invites.

The Common Bounce.—Of all the scoundrels that
stalk abroad in the world unhung for undetected enor-
mities, this is the most infamous I never had one of
this class pointed out to me in Dartmoor without
feeling a sort of longing for some Draconian law or

other that would rid mankind at once and for ever of
such monsters, and save human nature the shame of
having them appear clothed in the forms of men.   Yet
it is almost exclusively upon the same class of aged
victim as the one just described that these infamous
wretches ply their calling.   In a word, they train young
lads, generally thieves whom they are bringing out, to
follow such men—always, alas! old men—as they
believe to be "game," and endeavour to entice them
to some out-of-the-way place, where the scoundrel who
is watching pounces upon the victim, and, under a
threat of giving him into custody upon the most
abominable of all charges, obtains a sum of money

To do most professional thieves justice, they never
speak of these unique wretches except in terms the
most contemptible.

LECTURE XIV.

Provincial Thieves—Professional Jealousy—Foreign Thieves.

PROVINCIAL *Thieves.*—In the preceding sketches of
the various kinds of crime having representatives in
a convict prison, I have mostly confined my remarks
to the London and city types of thief, as they constitute
so large a proportion of the habitual criminal class of
Great Britain and Ireland, and are, especially those
from London, the most intellectual, successful, and
hardened of all offenders against the law. Liverpool,
Birmingham, Manchester, Glasgow, Leeds, and the
other large centres of population in the three countries
—each send their quota to the class of crimes which
I have enumerated; but very few of these extra-
London professors are equal to their metropolitan
brethren in artistic skill in the various methods of
theft employed. This is always a subject of boasting
to the Cockney jail-bird, but is not unfrequently re-
sented as an aspersion and an injustice by Liverpool

and Manchester burglars and pickpockets   The provincial thief has, as a rule, more natural intelligence,
if more war·ting in general knowledge of men and
things, than a Londoner, and is often found to have
followed some honest labour at one period of his life
Some exploits performed by Liverpool and Manchester
cracksmen have more than rivalled Cockney achievements in skill and daring ; and these deeds form a data
of fame upon which provincial boasters fall back when
it becomes a question of where "the best men" come
from.   Upon a young Manchester thief, who was employed in one of the parties to which I was attached in
Dartmoor, learning one day that I had resided for some
time near that city, he felt himself reinforced whenever London attempted to underrate the genius and
pluck of Manchester.   Controversies with Cockney
rivals were of almost daily occurrence, and taking it
for granted that I must be connected with the "profession" somehow, he argued as follows, on one occasion
" Can you " (addressing the Londoner) " show us " (himself and myself) " any job like the boning of the Pacha
of Egypt's jewelled sword when he was in Manchester ?
That was cleverness for you—wasn't it ? " (appealing
to me)   " Jack H——," he continued, " who was lately
in the Bank " (Millbank), " had a hand in that job,
and he's a smart un who can't be beat in all England.
Then there was the burst " (burglary) " at the watch-

maker's at the corner of Corporation Street, done by
little P—— D——, who boned 2,000*l.* worth of swag.
Tell us" (the speaker and myself) "where you Cocks
have beaten *that?*"

Notwithstanding such bright deeds as those just
boasted of, or of such as are not seldom performed by
Parisian and Dublin professors—the latter sometimes
considered more than the equals of the Londoners—the
Cockney thieves are unquestionably at the head of
the thieving profession in all its branches, as well as
being by far the most hardened and least amenable to
reformatory efforts of all criminals to be met with in
this country, or perhaps in any other part of the world.

Country Thieves—By this class of criminal is meant
such as are convicted from rural localities, as distinguishable from those who belong to provincial cities
and large towns. They are not largely represented in
convict society, owing, of course, to the absence in
country districts of the criminal-forming agencies such
as abound in London, as also the non-presence of
temptations to evil that are found principally where
luxury and wealthy idleness are fond of exhibiting
their riches.

They are the "bad characters" of a rural district
who have graduated in crime either through drinking
habits at the village alehouse, or from having received
one or two sentences in country prisons for poaching,

and learning, fiom association with professional thieves,
the career which generally ends in a sentence of penal
servitude. They are an unpopular class of men in a
convict prison, owing to their being quite at home in
such rough kind of manual labour as shovel, pick, or
barrow work—each and all of which kinds of occupation, as also any task requiring bodily exertion, are as
abhorrent to the entire city thieving classes as bacon
is to a Jew. By being able and willing to go through
their work easily they show up the idle propensities of
the other thieves in the party, and thereby beget an
antipathy which tends to still widen the breach between
the representatives of vulgar and civilised crime. They
are usually ignorant men, and nothing like as hardened
in crime as their city brethren. Very few of them are
ever re-convicted to penal servitude, as they either leave
the country when liberated, or join the army or navy.
As thieves they are of course held in the smallest
possible estimation by the accomplished city burglars
and hooks.

Foreign Thieves —A good sprinkling of French
and German, with some Italian thieves, are found in
all the large convict prisons, in almost every instance
convicted from London   They are far more intelligent
men and more enlightened than their English *confrères*
in crime   Some whom I have conversed with I have
found very well educated, speaking two or three

languages besides their own. As thieves they are poorly spoken of by the London professors, though from their superior intelligence and less criminally marked features and deportment I should incline to the belief that they are "men of mark" when at home. This is said more particularly of French thieves than of the other foreigners whom I have ranked with them. I am of opinion that very few could be found among even the most famed London hooks, who could "break off a jerry" in the following artistic manner, which bespeaks a *coup de génie* on the part of the Parisian professor of whom it has been often related.

An Englishman, exhibiting a large gold albert, and other "milor" marks of his wealth and insular importance, was one day patronising the Boulevard des Italiens, when he was respectfully saluted by an English-speaking, gentlemanly-looking native, with a "Would monsieur be so kind as to so far gratify the desire of a lady artist in an opposite window as to stand still for five seconds until she succeeds in taking a photograph of monsieur's face, which she declares exhibits beaucoup de caractère ?" "Oh, certainly, *monshure*, with the greatest possible pleasure!" was the response of the flattered Briton. "Just a little turn of monsieur's head, s'il vous plait. There, that will do. Mille remercîments. Bon jour, monsieur "— and "milor's" vanity lost him his watch.

LECTURE XV.

Miscellaneous Traits and Practices of Criminal Character—Demand for New Penal Legislation—Petitioning the Home Secretary—The Thief on "his Rights"—Malingering—Putting on the "Barmy Stick"—Diamond Cut Diamond—How to Detect Simulated Insanity—Mick Flanagan and the Lord Lieutenant of Ireland—Injury Done to *bona fide* Invalids by "Faiking"—Fatal Results to the Malingerers themselves.

THE foregoing classification of the criminal characters of a convict prison is not given as an absolutely correct one, but merely approximative of what the four conduct classes into which each prison is generally divided will embrace of the various types of criminal that prey upon society. Neither do these descriptive sketches of such types, and their respective *modus operandi* in the pursuit of theft, pretend to embrace either all the kinds of crime committed in these countries, or anything approaching to an illustration of all the schemes and ruses that are employed in their varied plundering avocations

Numbers of crimes are committed by men who are

met with in a prison, and which are talked of and boasted
of by them, which could not only not be mentioned
here, but which will not even allow of a hint of their
true nature to be breathed, so unmentionably foul and
loathsome are they. These crimes are seldom if ever
alluded to in police trials, as they constitute extra accomplishments or pursuits of beings so deeply sunk in
crime and shamelessness that their very souls seem to
be the essence of all that is filthy and abominable in a
beastly and degraded humanity. The tricks, dodges,
and other plans which I have sketched in my brief
descriptions of those who reply upon them for the
robbery of the public, constitute the principal and
most frequently employed schemes for resort to which
so many men are doomed to pass so great a portion of
their lives within the walls of a convict prison. There
is, of course, very little room in prisons like Portland,
Dartmoor, Portsmouth, or Millbank, for the exercise of
swindling, thieving, and other kindred practices of professional crime, and the observation of such strange
moral characters while under disciplinary restraint is
therefore a very interesting study. There is not among
any other class of men in this country to be found such
a constant talk of " rights," of " law," of " justice," and
of the Home Secretary, as is heard from those who for
the time being have forfeited almost all rights, who are
the avowed enemies of all law, and who know not what

justice is when they are defrauding or robbing confiding or unsuspecting victims While boasting of having committed crimes that were never brought to light, and while planning the perpetration of similar ones when they will be restored to liberty, these men, in the same breath, will inveigh against their convictions with genuine indignation, and threaten to expose judge, jury, detectives, and prison authorities for having acted contrary to law the moment they are in a position to do so before the public.

No party of reformers, social or political, dwell so much upon the absolute necessity there is for "a new Act" as the professional swindler and skilled pick-pocket. Scarcely a single batch of "new chums" (prisoners recently convicted) ever came to Dartmoor from Millbank, while I was in the former prison, who did not bring some cheering news of an impending revolution in the law relating to the convict world by the proximate introduction of a new Act into Parliament. At one time it would be promised legislation for shorter sentences and more gratuity upon discharge. Next, it might be the abolition of "the ticket," and the establishment of a penal colony somewhere in Africa; and again, an Act for the extension of good-conduct privileges, and an increase of rations. These supposed measures would be discussed at Sunday exercise as if their introduction into the

House had been fully determined upon by the Home
Secretary, and their passage into law a matter
of certainty

Every convict is permitted to petition the Secretary
of State upon any matter relative to his sentence or
treatment, and this privilege is very extensively availed
of by the intelligent portion of convicts.   In fact, so
numerous must these petitions be from the whole of
the convict prisons of England, that the reading of
them by him to whom they are addressed, if he were
compelled to do so, would require several hours a day
for the performance of the task.   Until the answer
arrives, the petitioner, in most instances, fully believes
that the Home Secretary is overhauling the records of
the trial, communicating with the judge who passed
sentence, and otherwise acquainting himself with all
the circumstances and bearings of the case that has
been laid before him by the convict petitioner.   But
should the answer prove unsatisfactory, it is simply
because " the Home Secretary has not seen the petition
at all, not a blooming line of it," or he would be sure to
do justice and reduce the sentence.   An individual who
would never be troubled by such a thing as conscience
in robbing another of all he might possess in the world
will threaten to bring the director and Secretary of
State down upon the whole prison staff if he thinks
there is an ounce of meat below the stipulated quantity

in his shin-of-beef soup, or if his loaf of bread should chance to be a fraction lighter than the weight mentioned in the rules as his due. "He knows his rights, and he'll have 'em too, or he'll see what somebody else has to say about the matter," &c., &c.

In order to gain some point upon which he has set his mind the professional thief will make any sacrifice, and scarcely stop at the doing of anything which he thinks may obtain the object of his desire. "Fetching the farm" (obtaining infirmary treatment) is the one thing in the lagging which the worst type of these men will strain every nerve and resort to every possible device that may be calculated to impose upon the doctor and other officials to get "Putting on the barmy stick" is one of the plans not unfrequently tried as a means of shirking labour and obtaining the relaxation of discipline and extra dietary treatment allowed by the medical officers to *bond fide* invalids. This consists in simulating madness, and in addition to the motives just mentioned it is often resorted to in hopes of securing a removal to some other prison. It very seldom happens that the prisoner succeeds in deceiving the doctor to the desired extent, as prisoners showing any symptoms of insanity are placed under special surveillance, which makes it well-nigh impossible for an impostor to deceive his watchers for any length of time.

Devices resorted to by convicts of this type for the purpose of "taking in the croaker," have begot detection dodges on the doctors' part also. One of these was described to me by an educated man who had "done a lagging" in C—— convict prison. Dr. ——, of that establishment, was noted for the number of fraudulent ailments which he had exposed as having been successfully passed off upon the medical officers of other prisons. Upon any convict showing symptoms of insanity, real or imaginary, he was at once placed under close observation. He would be located in an empty cell, and the first day's proceedings would commence by the administration of a powerful aperient disguised in some article of food. The patient would be then hurried into a warm bath, and, during the absence from his cell, an ordinary empty dinner-tin would be slipped inside the door, and the observations of the watching warder continued after the bathing was over. When the medicine began to operate, the patient would utilise the dinner-tin as the only utensil or convenient article to be found in his cell. This would all be noted, of course, through the spy-hole by the warder. Dinner time comes round. The tin is smuggled out of the cell without the act being noticed by the patient, and is, after a while, handed in again as if containing the rations of the prisoner. He is again closely watched. *If he eats of the contents, he is believed*

to be insane   If he does not, he is reported to the director
for a flogging for simulating madness

This system of detection was confined to C——
prison, and was only resorted to there by the doctor
alluded to ; but I am bound to say that no such abominable practice was adopted towards even known "barmy
stick" prisoners during my stay in Millbank, Dartmoor,
Portsmouth, or Portland.

These impostors will carry their acting to the extent
of inflicting wounds upon themselves, tearing and
smashing what can be thus destroyed, and behaving
in the most violent manner towards prisoners or
warders.

One of these, who was in Dartmoor during my
sojourn there, had almost gained his point and won a
recognition of his "insanity" from the doctor, so well
did he play his part, when he was caught on one
occasion endeavouring to get a look at the paper upon
which the warders were instructed to narrate the
proceedings and symptoms of the patient   As this
intelligent curiosity could scarcely be reconciled with
madness, "Barmy Flanagan," as he was termed, was
deservedly punished, and cured   He had been a soldier
in the British army ere enlisting in the thieving
service, and one of his dodges, while feigning madness,
was the writing of a letter to his grandmother in
Ireland, requesting her to "go and tell the Lord

Lieutenant that Mick Flanagan is in Dartmoor, and requests a visit from His Majesty in order to renew old acquaintance and be present when I make my will, as I intend to leave 5,000l. to the doctor for the kind treatment he has given me." Others cover themselves with their own filth and go through the most horrible actions in the hope of deceiving the medical officer, ending in nearly every instance by having ministered to their own suffering instead of obtaining the trivial luxuries for which all this heavy, self-inflicted punishment is undergone. This, like every other species of heartless imposture, leads to the injury of the poor wretches who really do become insane in prison, as it prolongs the period during which the prisoner exhibiting such symptoms must be kept under close observation in order to test the case, and when the "barmy sticks" are detected they are deservedly punished.

Another and more frequent means of "fetching the farm" is termed "faiking" (malingering), and like the previous kind of imposture is practised only by the lowest type of criminal, such as the pickpocket, bruiser, thief-cadger, and "Her Majesty's bad bargains" —as soldier-convicts are called by the other prisoners. As these are all more or less inoculated with the worst forms of bodily disease, it becomes an easy task for such prisoners to so tamper with themselves as to compel medical treatment to be given them. Among

the most common methods of doing this is the pro-
curing of inflammation of some part of the arms, legs,
feet, face, or eyes, by the infliction of some slight injury
and then applying a piece of copper-wire, or other
inflaming agent, that will cause the wounded flesh
to swell or fester.   Scores of other plans are likewise
employed to the same end, often resulting in the
infliction of a permanent injury, and not unfrequently
purchasing premature death for some who act thus
criminally towards their bodily health.   Characters who
are noted for this kind of prison fraud are very unpopular among the majority of prisoners, as the
prevalence of this practice of "faiking" begets a
suspicion in the doctor's mind of the genuineness of
nearly all ailments and accidents that, of course, are as
incidental to those who labour inside as to those who
are employed outside prison walls, and thereby subjects
those who are suffering from them to unmerited
suspicion and the danger of neglect.

LECTURE XVI.

CRIMINAL VANITY

Inscriptions on the Walls of "the Waiting-for-Sentence Cell" in Newgate—The Love-Letter—*Slang:* Specimen Thieves' Latin—Key to same.

THAT weakness or vanity which induces travellers to carve their names upon the Pyramids, rocks, or stones near famous sites, walls of Roman and other historic ruins, religious shrines and birthplaces of poets, is very largely developed in criminal character. I recollect having occupied the half-hour during which the jury was considering whether to believe the evidence of respectable witnesses or accept that of a creature who can be truly designated a salaried perjurer in my respect, in reading the inscriptions which covered the walls of the cell—the waiting-room of Fate—in Newgate Prison, to which I was conducted while my future was being decided in the jury-room overhead. Every available inch of the blackened mortar contained, in

few words, the name of the writer, where he belonged
to, the crime with which he was charged, the dread
certainty of conviction, the palpitating hopes of
acquittal, or the language of indifference or despair.
What thoughts must have swept through the minds
of the thousands who have passed through that cell,
during the necessarily brief stay within its walls ! Loss
of home, friends, reputation, honour, name—to those
who had such to lose ; and the impending sentence of
banishment from the world of pleasure or business
for years—perhaps for ever—with the doom of penal
degradation, toil, and suffering in addition !

Yet, despite all these feelings that crowd upon the
soul in these short, fleeting, terrible moments of
criminal life, the vanity—or what shall I term it ?—of
the individual prompts him to occupy most of them in
giving a short record of himself, his crime or imputed
offence, scratched upon these blackened walls, for other
succeeding unfortunates to read !

Most of these inscriptions were in slang, showing
that the majority of those who had written them were
of the criminal order, and guilty of some, if not of the
particular offence for which they were doomed to await
the announcement of their punishment within that
chamber of dread expectancy   Not a few, however,
consisted of declarations of innocence, invocations of
Divine interposition, appeals to Justice, and confidence

in the " laws of my country ," while others denoted the
absence of all thoughts except those of wife, children, or
sweetheart. Some who were awaiting that most terrible
of all sentences—death—could yet think of tracing the
outlines of a scaffold amidst the mass of surrounding
inscriptions, with a "Farewell to life" scrawled underneath. Giving way to the seeming inspiration of the
place, and picturing jurors' faces round that dismal den
—dark and frowning—into which the sun's rays never
entered, lit only by a noisy jet of gas which seemed to
sing the death-song of the liberty of all who entered
the walls which it had blackened—I stood upon the
form which extended round the place, and wrote upon
a yet uncovered portion of the low sloping roof—

"M. D. expects ten years for the crime of being an Irish
Nationalist and the victim of an informer's perjury.

"*July*, 1870."

From the ghastly look of the cell, the penalty I was
about to undergo, and my own thoughts at the moment,
I might have most appropriately added the well-known
lines from the *Inferno*, which invite those who enter
its portals of despair to abandon hope.

Not only on the walls of that never-to-be-forgotten
black hole, but on the cell-walls and doors in all
my subsequent wanderings in penal life—in Millbank,
Dartmoor, Portsmouth, and Portland—have I spent

hours in deciphering the records of "famous" deeds and particular "professions," dates of sentences and the penalties awarded to the strange beings who had preceded me along that slow, weary, and heartsore journey of punishment.

Fuller accounts of the professions and proficiency of the occupants would be sure to be always found upon the cell slate, written by them for the envious admiration of the prisoner who was next to be located there. These histories, invariably written in slang, have afforded me much amusement at times, and have been a means, among others, of aiding me in the mastery of the criminal vocabulary, which I have so frequently used in these sketches.

Young thieves would, of course, "blow their own horn" in narrating their sentences and exploits, by taking credit for imaginary deeds of fame, not "honestly" acquired, but old hands could be easily traced in the terse expressions which would record—

"A burst in the City. Copped while boning the swag. 7 stretch, 1869. Roll on 1876. Cheer up, pals."
Another—
"Hook. 7 ys. Roll on time"
Another—
"Bob White from the Dials 5 stretch for slugging a copper."

"Little Dickey from the New Cut. 10 and a ticket Put away by a moll" (sold by an unfortunate).

And such like information, on through the whole category of crime.

The great majority of convicts hide their real under assumed names, many of them having a fresh "monicker" (name) each conviction, to be dropped, for obvious reasons, upon release. The giving of names, therefore, in these sketches, reveals nothing that would injure the persons who were the bearers while undergoing their "laggings."

A letter, of which the following is an exact copy, was left by a prisoner in one of the cells which I occupied after receiving sentence in Newgate. It afforded much amusement to the officers of that prison, who kept it in that particular cell, and who called my attention to it upon my removal thereto, in order, I believe, to distract my mind from the sentence that had been passed upon me a couple of days previously.

"Shor ditch — 1870.

"DEERE JIM

"i was in quod, doin 14 days when i heerd you was lagged i blakked Polly S——'s peepers who called me names she was fuddled and hit me fust, when i kolered her nut and giv her a fine slugging and her mug was all over blud the spiteful thing bit me she did, and funked fight, when we were both taken by the Kopper, and the beek only giv me 14 days, and her got 21 for hitten me fust and been fuddled, cheer up Jim i am sorry wot you are lagged, and i wont pal with nobody wile your in quod. good by Jim from your tru luv   SALLY."

Whether this is the fair one whom the song of the period described—

"Her fighting weight was thirteen stone,
And her maiden name was Sarah,"

I know not, but her love-letter to poor Jim was the means of eliciting from me the first laugh in which I felt inclined to indulge in that early stage of penal servitude.

Slang—A pickpocket told me the history of his arrest one day in the following language:—

"I was jogging down a blooming slum in the Chapel when I butted a reeler who was sporting a red slang I broke off his jerry and boned the clock, which was a red one, but I was spotted by a copper who claimed me I was lugged before the beak, who gave me six doss in the Steel. The week after I was chucked up I did a snatch near St. Paul's, was collared, lagged, and got this bit of seven stretch."

In English this would read as follows:—

"As I was walking down a narrow alley in Whitechapel I ran up against a drunken man who had a gold watch-guard. I stole his watch, which was gold, but was seen by a policeman, who caught me and took me before the magistrate, who gave me six months in the Bastille [Middlesex House of Detention, so named by thieves]. When I was released I attempted to steal a watch near St. Paul's, but was taken again, convicted, and sentenced to seven years' penal servitude."

The use of slang in prisons is prevalent only among the lower order of thieves, but is, of course, employed by all habitual criminals when in company, or on the theft path outside. Some of the pickpocket fraternity are so addicted to it that their true character might be inferred from its almost constant presence in their conversation.

Thieves' Latin.—This improvement upon slang is more a special criminal method of speech than the ordinary slang, and is of general use among the professional burglar and "hook" orders of thief when in pursuit of game. Its chief peculiarity consists in reversing the position of the syllables of a word containing more than one syllable, and making two syllables of all words having only one in ordinary pronunciation by adding a vowel or liquid consonant to the first or second part of such word. By the application of this simple rule to slang words the "lingo" becomes too complicated for any but the initiated to understand. For instance, if two thieves were prowling for game, and one were to see a policeman, he would shout to his comrade—

"Islema! Ogda the opperca!" which in slang is—"Misle! Dog the copper!" otherwise—"Vanish! See the policeman!"

If a pair of confederates were in company with some
"flat," or easily-deceived person whom they were about
to fleece, the lingo would be used as a means by which
they would intercommunicate their impressions of the
victim in his hearing, and give directions what was
best to do in order to obtain his money—

"A uffma, ill olloswa a alewha. Itchpa the idesna,
or utpo the ukedo in the obfa," would be some of the
phrases needed for such an emergency

In ordinary slang the foregoing would stand as
follows—"He is a muff, and will swallow a whale.
Pitch the snide, or put your duke in his fob;" and
translated into English would read—"He is such a
confounded ass that he will stand almost anything
Try the counterfeit coin, or pick his pocket"

As some words will not admit very well of the
necessary transposition of syllables needed to disguise
the talk from listening victims or enemies, the first
syllables of such words, if immediately following each
other, will change places, so that the first syllable, letter,
or letters of the second word will become that or those
of the first word, and *vice-versâ* For instance, if Jack
had made the discovery that a person whom himself
and Bill were following had only a silver watch, the
disgusting fact would be told to Jack as follows —

"I jay, Sack, the okeblo's wack's clite;" which in
slang would be—"I say, Jack, the bloke's clock is only

a white one ," and in English—"The fellow's watch is only silver "

The letters "J " and "s" of the words "Jack" and "say" are exchanged; the ordinary lingo rule is followed in reference to the word "bloke" and the "cl" of the word "clock," and "w" of "white" are exchanged as in the case of the letters "J " and "s."

LECTURE XVII.

PRISON "POETS."

Chateaubriand's Theory—Effective Criticism of the Governor—
The Creative Muses of Newgate, Millbank, Dartmoor, and
Portsmouth—Circumscribed nature of the Poet's Oppor-
tunities—Jones, his Lucy, and the Critic—Unwarranted
Poetic Licence—Crutchy Quinn Celebrates Seven Prisons—
—His Autobiography—The Millbank Poet who Beat Shake-
speare—His subsequent more congenial Exploits in Dublin
—A Portsmouth School of Poetry—The Muse among Bricks
—A Bread and Water Criticism.

PRISON *Poets.*—I am not about to include in this
lecture the mighty muse of a Tasso, or the amorous
elegances of a Lovelace or a Waller, or other distinguished patrons of Pegasus who may have strung
their lyres and sent f th tuneful song while held in
durance vile. My votaries of that steed of song are, as
yet, entirely unknown to poetic fame, and I very much
fear that such of their performances as a treacherous
memory will permit me to rescue from the tablets of

cell-doors, skilly-cans, bottoms of dinner-tins, and the less oblivious pages of whitewashed walls, will scarcely rank them among the inspired community of immortal songsters.

Chateaubriand has remarked that man or bird is never so prone to sing as when caged. Whether this be really so or not I cannot venture to say, but certain I am that the criminal " muse " would never be heard, if—

> " Stone walls did *not* a prison make
> Nor iron bars a cage "

for jail-bird " poets." The " poetry " of prison walls, cell-doors, slates, can-bottoms, tin knives, and margins of books must, in the first place, be necessarily of a fragmentary nature, and be wanting in that descriptive power which would require for its exposition more stanzas than one, or more lines than from four to twelve—the ordinary range of most poetic flights of convict genius. In almost every other respect it must also suffer in the important point of execution, owing, chiefly, to the fact that all such performances, no matter how truly inspired or instinctive with condensed thought or beauty, are held to be by prison critics—that is, warders—" defacing " the walls, doors, &c., and are made a vulgar question of bread and water to the hungry author when translated on a slip of paper in the form of a report for the final opinion of

that stern reviewer, the governor There is no pro-
hibition, however, in regard to the use of a slate, but
unfortunately my reading has been almost exclusively
confined to the contents of the former more circumscribed mediums of written convict song I noticed
that Clerkenwell House of Detention failed to evoke a
single poetic sentiment, or to stir a particle of the
divine fire in its inmates, while *in transitu* to liberty or
other stage of imprisonment Newgate gave birth to
but a very selfish sentimentality or the severely sarcastic,
notwithstanding its historic record Millbank seemed
to inspire a livelier strain, with wider sympathies,
while the sarcasm which it also evoked was a means
by which disappointed gourmands revenged themselves
upon the culinary *chef* of that famous establishment
Dartmoor and Portsmouth gave each their peculiar
idiosyncrasies to the widening stream of breathing
thought and burning word This poetic development
in proportion to the degrees of captivity represented
by the foregoing stages of waiting trial, conviction, probationary existence, and the full creative influence of
heavier tasks and fuller rations, with correspondingly
growing experiences of Chateaubriand's cage, seems
to bear out that famous writer's theory in a very
conclusive manner

The first book which I was given to read in Newgate
had been in the hands of two poets of an opposite

school of feeling when inditing their respective contributions to the spare margins of that volume. The first,
who was evidently of the sentimental class, poor fellow,
had written—"Good-bye, Lucy dear," throughout the
book, upwards of as many times as the love-smitten
hero of *As You Like It* had carved the name of Rosalind
on the trees of Arden Forest, ere he ventured to clothe
his feelings in more musical language, but finally
dashed off—

> " Good-bye, Lucy dear,
>   I'm parted from you for seven long year
>   "ALF JONES "

This modest performance, to which the lamenting
poet courageously affixed his name, contained a story of
love and misfortune, and should, on that account alone,
have appealed to the charitable criticism of all who
might read the same   But right underneath this effort
of the love-sick Jones, a sour and sceptical ...ffrey had
added the following verse.—

> " If Lucy dear is like most gals,
>   She ll give few sighs or moans,
>   But soon will find among your pals
>   Another Afred Jones."

Like all unmerciful critics, this heartless wretch, who
was evidently himself a sufferer from some fair one's
slight, or perhaps evidence, refused to attach his name
to his contribution, but fortunately for Lucy's *inamorato*

the stigma which was thus cast upon her constancy and that of her whole sex would fall under his notice only in case of his losing Lucy again after liberation and passing through Newgate in the course of a second lagging.

The next original effusion which met my eye in Newgate, also in the sentimental strain, though of a bolder sweep than that of the poet Jones, was as follows :—

"The judge he seven years gave me, transported to Van Diemen's Land,
Far away from my friends and relations, and the girl with the
  ˙rk velvet band."

Now, inasmuch as these lines were written in the city of London in 1869, and that neither thieves nor poets ..e now transported from England to any more distant region of the world than Dartmoor, the second line of this verse amounts to a most unwarranted stretch of poetic licence, being introduced only to find a rhyme for the sable ornament of the writer's lady love À propos of the description which we find given of this lady, was she the only girl in existence with a dark velvet band ? and did she wear it round her neck, or arm, or —but, impossible !—was it akin to the sacred ornament which gave rise to the legend, "*Honi soit qui mal y pense*" ?   Well for the writer that he neglected to affix his name to such a production, as the poetic censor who cut up Jones and his Lucy would have emptied all his wrath upon the anonymous writer's style and taste.

My next selection will be from the muse of Millbank, who, in consequence of change of scenery and the more advanced march of the poets on the song-inspiring journey of penal servitude, is of a more epicurean turn than her sentimental sister at Newgate Margins of books are no longer available, however, for the preservation of amorous verse or sorrowing ditty, for reasons already hinted at, and the substitutes must become as various as the objects celebrated. On the bottom of a dinner-can, and written with a nail, I discovered the following :—

> " *Millbank* for thick shins and graft at the pump ;
> *Broadmoor* for all laggs as go off their chump ,
> *Brixton* for good toke and cocoa with fat ;
> *Dartmoor* for bad grub but plenty of chat ;
> *Portsmouth* a blooming bad place for hard work ,
> *Chatham* on Sunday gives four ounce of pork ;
> *Portland* is worst of the lot for to joke in—
> For fetching a lagging there is no place like *Woking*
>   "CRUTCHY QUINN, 16 and ticket."

In one respect this short, but very descriptive poem appeared to have something of a pretence to more crime than would give a prison experience sufficient to cover so much ground as eight convict establishments; but as I had the distinguished privilege of not only meeting the poet "Crutchy," but of occupying a cell next to his in Dartmoor a twelve-month after reading the above, I discovered that he had really passed some portion of time in seven of the prisons whose praise or shortcomings he had so graphically described while doing his "separates" in Millbank for the third time.

His Celtic patronymic reminds me that I have so far left you in complete ignorance as to what is the nationality of prison poets, or in what proportion, rather, they are distributable between England, Scotland, Wales, and Ireland. I am a firm believer in the wisdom of the German proverb, that "Neither one's country nor mankind is served by national vanity," and I have, therefore, throughout the whole of these lectures, claimed so very little of professional or poetic genius for my own country, that I am in no fear of being charged with any undue partiality I am, however, in obedience to the behest of truth, compelled to give two-thirds of the prison poets to the land of Moore

Crutchy Quinn, despite his surname, I found to be a Saxon, though his own story, told to me as follows, would lead to consistency with his name —

"I am the brother of the celebrated Corporal Quinn, who took a company of Russians prisoners by his own bravery in the Crimea   an inventor, and to my love for the study of invention is due this, my misfortune. I once made a model of a patent diving-bell which would surpass anything of the sort ever invented before I showed it to a gentleman in London, who had something of the same sort in his nut also. Seeing that my plan was the best, he resolved to put me away, and he did it in this manner: I was walking down Cheapside one day, when this rascal meets me, and asks my opinion of a gold chronometer which he had just purchased for twenty quid. No sooner did I take the watch in my hand than he shouted for a copper, and gave me into custody for attempting to steal it from him ! Did you ever hear of such villainy before in broad daylight?" Upon repeating this story, a few days after having heard it, to a London pickpocket who "knew everybody," he gave me the following as the true history of Crutchy ·—"That is all one of Crutchy's blooming yarns He has been here twice before, and had a new monicker each time He is not Irish, but a born Cockney, and when he has done this bit he will have spent twenty-five years of his life in quod" Crutchy sustained his reputation as a poet during the time he and I were fellow-prisoners in Dartmoor.

But returning to Millbank There can be no doubt as to the country that gave birth to the author of the follo   sad couplet, which I found very

appropriately inscribed upon one of the tin knives
in that prison —

"I had for my dinner, ochone! ochone!
One ounce of mutton and three ounce of bone!"

It was while studying the backs of doors and the
bottoms of dinner-cans in this establishment, that I
first met a convict poet in the flesh. He did me the
honour of requesting me to become the critic of a piece
of blank verse, which, he declared, had elicited from the
schoolmaster an opinion that Shakespeare had nothing
equal to it in any of is works. I, of course, suddenly
became deeply interested in the individual who could
beat Shakespeare hollow, and asked how I could have
the pleasure of reading his lines. "Oh, exchange
slates," he replied "Nothing easier. We can do it
in the morning when the gates are unlocked for chapel"
This conversation occurred while returning from
prayers; so on the following morning I became possessed of his slate, and found about fifty lines of a
medley, which commenced with

"When most alone we are least alone,"

containing nothing but a string of unconnected lines
stolen from Milton Shakespeare, and Young's *Night
Thoughts* This was discouraging, and would scarcely
have earned for Shakespeare's rival a place among my

co t poets if I had not met him again under any-
thi but poetic circumstances Nine years after this
incident I was walking along Stephen's Green, in
Dublin, one evening, when who should I see coming
in an opposite direction, in company with two more
individuals, but the well-remembered face of the man
who claimed to have beaten the Swan of Avon in Millbank. As I had learned, while his associate in this
penitentiary, of his more congenial accomplishments, I
ventured to predict to the friend with whom I was
chatting when this *rencontre* occurred, that some clever
burglary or cheat would take place in Dublin ere many
days had gone by. Two days afterwards the whole city
was thrown into a state of excitement in consequence of
numbers of forged 10l. National Bank notes having
been successfully tendered to various shopkeepers and
dealers ere their counterfeit character was discovered.
One of the "snide pitchers" was caught, but he was
not the leader of the gang—my quondam poetic neighbour of Millbank, doubtless, who had made good his
escape, but if he had been caught and subjected to
the poetic inspiration of Spike Island, he would, to a
certainty, soon aspire to take the laurels from the brow
of the author of the Melodies.

As Dartmoor was, poetically speaking, in possession
of Cutchy Quinn during the whole of my sojourn in

that place, truly famous for "bad grub," if not for
"plenty of chat," and as I have already given a
sample of his poetry, I must pass on to Portsmouth
prison, which, from some cause or other never satisfac-
torily explained, had the reputation of numbering more
poets among its criminal population than all the other
convict prisons combined.   I was told by one of these
geniuses that the schoolmaster encouraged poetry among
prisoners, and that once a fortnight, on book-changing
days, each votary of the Portsmouth muse would
leave his composition on his slate where the prison
Holofernes could read it and mark his approval or
other opinion for the perusal of the author.   This appeal   to me as simply exquisite; and I looked forward
to a long and constant enjoyment of this community of
imprisoned songsters, when, unfortunately for the remainder of this lecture on prison poets, I was sent
back to Dartmoor with only a few weeks experience of
my new acquaintances   Short as my stay in Portsmouth
was, however, it was not altogether barren of poetic
results   Upon reaching the place where my gang
was employed, one morning in the July of 1872, the
officer in charge bade me go to the end stack of bricks,
and the prisoner who was there at work would teach
me how to "skintle," i e stack wet bricks   The
personage to whose teaching I was thus c   ed was a

little n of fifty or more years of age. Having eyed
me very closely on my approach, he saluted me with
the startling question, " Are you a *pôte ?* "

Somewhat taken aback at the thought that there
might be some connection between the composition of
poetry and the manufacture of bricks hitherto undreamt
of by me, I answered, " No ! " " I am " was the proud
and prompt reply. " Indeed ! " I ventured to observe,
" and have you published any works ? " " No, but I
have made a lot of poetry," he answered in a tone that
might have plied to so many barrow-loads of bricks.
' Upon wh. subjects have you chiefly composed ? "
was my next inquiry. " The pugging machine—"
" ut what is that, please ? " I interrupted. " That is
what makes the bricks," was the reply. " Holy Joe."
' Who is he, pray ? " " Oh ! that is our chaplain."
" Well ? " " I have made some poetry on Pentonville
too," he continued, and immediately putting himself
in an attitude of poetic frenzy, he recited—

> " 'Twas one fine morning I left Wakefield Jail,
> Meself and comrades we did cry our fill,
> Far from our friends we were now transported
> Till the same evening we rached Pentonville—"

" If you don't stop that jaw, Horgan, and allow that
man to go on with his work, I'll give you a run ! " broke
in the anything-but-musical voice of the warder upon

the poet and startled auditor; and as the threatened "run," if carried out, would entail more disagreeable consequences than the combined critical condemnation of all the literary reviews, there was no more "poetry" recited that day

LECTURE XVIII.

DESPAIR AND HOPE IN PRISON.

Fortitude of ordinary Convicts—Effects of "Solitary" at be-
ginning of Sentence—Millbank and Big Ben—Horrible
Consciousness of Slow March of Sentence—An Instance of
Sudden Madness—Death from Want of Hope—A Midnight
Tale of Heart-sorrow—A Murderer's extraordinary Hope
—Story of Drunkenness and Murder—Convict Castle-
builders

As it seldom happens that even the worst of criminals
is found to be all crime, neither is an association of
one thousand of convicts all repulsive moral deformity.
Imprisonment, like many other unfortunate occurrences
in the life of those who are born under an unlucky star,
has what, for want of a more accurate expression, I
shall term its bright side also, inasmuch as its life in
some very remote respects approaches to that of the less
criminal—because unconvicted—outside world All the
talk of a convict prison is not of murder, theft, and
indecency, nor is misery and unhappiness always present

among those who may be supposed to be the exclusive
victims of "grim-visaged Despair." Therefore is there
what I may call a negative silver lining to even the
dark cloud of penal existence. It is a most singular
thing that I have met very few individuals in prison
who gave evidence, in appearance or talk, of being
truly miserable, no matter what the length of their
sentence, amount of extra punishment, or contrast
between their previous and their convict life, may have
been. It is true the deepest sorrow and most acute
pains of life are often hid from the mockery of human
pity away in the recesses of the sufferer's breast, and
that therefore the smiling face and cheerful conversation
are not to be relied upon as sure indications of a con-
tented or happy existence. Yet a constant and familiar
observation of men of all ages, possessing the stongest
of human passions while being subject to disciplinary
restraints that have no parallel in the daily annoyance
or troubles of outside life, would be almost certain to
detect any tendency towards despair or severe heart-
suffering on the part of men who should succomb to
their fate or surroundings. It is also certain that
numbers of prisoners having comfortable homes in the
outer world must often indulge in sad regrets for what
has lost them their enjoyment, and allow their minds
to dwell on the painful contrast between the, perhaps,
happy influence and remembrance of the one, and the

cheerless and weary aspect of the other mode of life.
But these feelings are seldom or ever exhibited in the
general behaviour or talk of four-fifths of the inmates
of a convict prison; and happy, indeed, is it for all concerned in their custody that it is so, as such a mass of
bridled passions, if maddened by ever-present thoughts
of family, home, and former pleasures (while mind and
body are made conscious every hour in every day of the
terrible penalties which crime has purchased), would
become as unmanageable and dangerously restless as a
thousand caged hyenas.

It is only when these possible feelings overcome the
resisting influence of Hope and Patience—the bright
and ever-present guardian angels of the imprisoned—
nowhere so needed, and, thanks to a beneficent Provi-
dence, nowhere so constantly present and powerful as in
a prison—that the heart fails in presence of seemingly
unbearable woe, inducing mental aberration and finally
insanity in the unfortunate victims. Such cases are,
however, not frequent, while the instances of prisoners
buoying up their existence under the weight of *life*
sentences with the hope of something being done for
them some time, through the agency of some fortunate circumstance or other, are almost as numerous as
are such terrible sentences themselves.

The first two years of penal servitude are the hardest
to bear, and test mental endurance more than the whole

of the remainder of an ordinary sentence. Liberty has only just been parted with. The picture of the outside world is still imprinted upon the memory, and home and friends, with perhaps a dearer object still, are made to haunt the recollection whenever the association of ideas recalls some incidents of happier days. Of these two years the heaviest portion is comprised within the nine or ten months which must be spent in what is termed "probation"—solitary confinement in Millbank or Pentonville; and while "solitary" is not much dreaded by ordinary prisoners at a later stage of penal existence, it is truly a terrible ordeal to undergo at the commencement. In Millbank this is specially so. The prison is but a few hundred yards west of Westminster Palace, from whence comes, every quarter of an hour, the voice of Big Ben, telling the listening inmates of the penitentiary that another fifteen minutes of their sentences have gone by! What horrible punishment has not that clock added to many an unfortunate wretch's fate, by counting for him *the minutes* during which stone walls and iron bars *will* a prison make! Then again there are the thousand and one noises that penetrate the lonely cells and silent corridors of that cheerless abode   Now it is the strains of a band from St James's Park, "bringing back to the memory merry days long gone by;" next it is the whistle of the railway engine, with its suggestiveness of a journey "home;"

and so on, during the long weary days and nights, and the terrible idea of suicide is forced across the mind as the only mode of release from the horrible mad   of the noisy, joyful world beyond the boundary walls

It is not surprising that many men have gone mad in Millbank. I was but a few weeks an inmate when I had to witness a sad incident of the kind. We were at prayers one morning in the Catholic chapel, and the choir, made up of prisoners, was singing one of Father Faber's beautiful supplications to the Virgin Mother. The air to which the words were sung was one of joyousness and hope, such as would easily cause a listener to travel back to the schoolboy period of life, and dwell again on a time ere prisons or suffering were much thought of Suddenly a wild, heart-bursting cry rang out above the voices of the singers, from a convict of some forty-five years of age, a few seats removed from where I was seated. He rushed towards the altar with piercing shrieks, while his eyes and face proclaimed the sudden loss of reason and the presence of madness. I thought at the time that the hymn, or the air to which it was being sung, might have brought up to the wretched man's memory the voices of his children and the thought of the years that must elapse—years of penal servitude, too—before he could again see or hear them, and that under this frightful strain upon the mind and heart he suddenly became a raving maniac.

Two instances of somewhat more natural, but scarcely less tragic consequences, comprise the number of cases in which I have observed the evidence of overmastering despair in convict life   In the early years of my sen- ~nce, in Dartmoor, I became acquainted with a very quiet and very intelligent prisoner named Howard, who bore a most excellent character, as far as prison conduct could show.   His story was indeed a sad one.   He was upwards of sixty years of age, and had resided in Liver- pool mostly all his life.   His wife had been a confirmed drunkard for years, from which circumstance it was easy to credit his assertion that their marriage had been an unhappy one, and his life a misery in consequence. He came home from his work one evening to discover that she had pawned some article of furniture in order to obtain money for more drink, whereupon an alter- cation ensued, which caused the wretched woman to rush from the room and tumble down a flight of stairs, at the bottom of which she was found with a broken neck.   Overcome with remorse at the thought that his scolding had been the cause of her fall, Howard was overheard by two women to exclaim, in agony, "My God! I have killed my wife!" This was given in evidence against him at the subsequent inquest and trial, and he was sentenced to penal servitude for life. Conscious of his innocence of the crime of murder, and relying upon his former good character and exemplary prison behaviour, he was confident that he would obtain his liberation after three years' imprisonment He petitioned the Home Secretary, told his story, and awaited the reply, which he fully believed would see him again a free man The reply came in due time: the Secretary of State saw no grounds for interfering with the sentence of the judge Within a month after the receipt of this second sentence to his cherished hope, Howard was freed by death from the life of penal servitude.

The remaining instance had not so fatal an ending.

I was kept awake late one summer night in 1874 by the unusual spectacle of the moon's rays penetrating through my cell window. It was the first time I had had such a visitor during four years, and the circumstance had touched a chord of memory and set the mind upon a train of thought which was not friendly to repose. The night-guard, in muffled tread, had glided past my door like a ghostly shadow, and all was as still within the prison as the midnight silence of a churchyard. From beyond the walls there came, at intervals, the barking of some farmer's dog, as if my new-found lamp of night were keeping him awake also, and in the midst of this stillness, at an hour when—

> "Sleep on its downy pinions flies from woe
> To light on lids unsullied by a tear,"

a timid knock was given to the partition which divided

my cell from the next prisoner, and an eager, sobbing voice exclaimed, "Can *you*, dear sir, tell me if Mary *is* dead?" Startled at the intensity of suffering which could prompt so heart-breaking an appeal for information from a complete stranger, I found it impossible to reply, until I heard again, as if in answer to my silence, "Ah, yes! she *must* be dead. My God! what will become of my children!" No matter how little a heart may be attuned to human sympathy, it must partake more or less of the agony which makes a strong man writhe in pain; and the knowledge which my unknown neighbour's question gave me of suffering so near to me, and so far surpassing that upon which I had been selfishly ruminating that night, chased all thoughts of sleep from my mind. I soon learned the history of the stranger's life, and the cause of his heartache. He had but arrived in Dartmoor from Millbank a few days previous to the incident just related, and was only a year in prison altogether. He had been a stonemason in Wales before getting into trouble, and the cause of his imprisonment was this. He came home from work one Saturday evening "a little fresh," but not drunk, and finding his wife in tears he demanded what was the matter, and was told by his eldest child, a girl seven years old, that a man who lived across the street had insulted her mother. Morris, the name of the man of whom this is related, rushed out with a chisel in his

Land and attacked the person who had offered insult to his wife, leaving him desperately wounded in his own house. For this he was tried and sentenced to seven years' penal servitude; and from the day of conviction until the night on which he recounted to me his sorrows he had heard no word from or of his wife or children. I never knew that man to smile during the time he spent in Dartmoor. His existence seemed to be one perpetual sorrow, and he formed altogether the most striking exception to the rule of non-despairing prisoners which came under my notice during my long intercourse with Dartmoor's criminal population.

The contrary feeling of hope is the prevailing one among prisoners, especially among those having long sentences. The less reasonable the cause for clinging to what is often but a straw in the sea of desperation, the more tenacious is the hold that is kept of it. One such instance has struck me as being a most remarkable evidence of hope being a providential gift with the power of saving reason, and often life, when everything else appears to abandon both to melancholy, madness, or death, and may be mentioned here as a sample of what tends to keep despair at bay within the walls of a convict prison.

In the second party to which I was attached for

labour in Dartmoor, was a man named Slack, a very quiet, intelligent, and remarkably well-conducted prisoner, who had at that period (1873) completed seven years of a sentence of twenty without having had a single report marked against him for misbehaviour of any kind. His crime was the murder of his wife, who, from his own apparently truthful statement, was the worst of bad life-partners, an habitual drunkard He had been the owner of two or three canal-boats and other property in the neighbourhood of D———, and as fast as he could earn money his wife would squander it in drink. He finally went on the spree also, came home drunk one night, and, in a quarrel that ensued, committed the horrible offence for which he was sentenced to twenty years' imprisonment. In fact, he admitted he had got drunk purposely with the intention of doing under the influence of drink what he had not the conscience to attempt when sober —to rid himself of his sot of a wife. There must have been extenuating circumstances in the case, or Slack would have been sentenced to the gallows. He made over all his property in charge to his brother until he should be liberated, leaving with it the task of endeavouring to obtain either his release or a reduction of his sentence from the Home Secretary. After the completion of one year he received a short letter from his brother counselling hope, and telling him not to expect any further communication until there would be some good news to send, hoping that that would not be long.

"And have you not heard from your brother these six years?" I asked one day, after listening to his story of drink, murder, and repentance.

"Oh, no," he replied. "Did not he say I need not expect to have a letter again until he could send a good one? I am expecting one now every day, and I think that as I have just finished seven years the Secretary of State will send me my release, coming on Christmas."

Shortly after this conversation Slack was removed to some other prison, and I lost sight of him for a little over five long years more, when he turned up again in Dartmoor, through being included in a batch of transfers from Portsmouth, to which prison he had been previously removed. A few weeks before the realisation of my own long-cherished hopes I met Slack one Sunday at exercise, and upon inquiring if he had any expectation of release, he repeated, almost word for word, the reply he had made to a similar question five years earlier, adding only, "As I have done *twelve years* now without a report, I am certain the Secretary of State will soon discharge me." If that unfortunate

N 2

wretch was told what those who listened to his story believed of his brother's conduct, he would probably have been released by death ere he had served half the term he had then been in prison.

This all-sustaining prison virtue, Hope, necessarily begets a kindred sort of comforting delusion in prisoners, adapting itself to the seeming requirements of those whose lot is hardest, and hiding the worst features of the objective present behind a picture of a pleasant and happy, if imaginary, future. Prison is the paradise of castle-builders—the fruitful dream-land of fortunes to be made, happiness to be won, and pleasures to be tasted, that shall more than compensate for the trials and privations of the past by the double enjoyment of their intrinsic delights and the contrast which their possession will make to the days when prison walls had frowned upon liberty and prison rations had but little comparison with the food of the gods. Alnaschar himself never conjured up so glorious a picture of gratification that was to come as will the imaginative convict while employed at his daily task, or in confiding his plans and prospects of the future to some one who will lend an attentive ear to their narration. Apart from such of the airy structures as are erected upon projected crime, this phase of criminal mental activity often conducts the stream of convict talk from its ordinary track on ugly themes into a more pleasant channel, in which it is easy to learn something of the better side of those whose blacker deeds and criminal ideas I have already endeavoured to sketch.

LECTURE XIX

CONVICT READING AND FAVOURITE LITERATURE

Influence of Literature upon Criminal Minds—Suggestions for a Prison Library—Criminal Aversion to direct Religious or Moral Teaching—The Periodical Literature of a Prison Library—The Religion of Criminals in Prison.

THE novel, and works of travel, with the varied reading of such magazines as are permitted into a prison library, are the favourite selections of convicts; and as none of the sensational or questionably moral kind of the former branch of English literature are allowed inside a prison, the influence for good which the higher class of such works might be capable of exercising upon almost morally deadened heads and hearts is scarcely appreciated by those of the public who question the wisdom and lenity of allowing convicts the privilege of reading romances. In my opinion no more efficacious reforming medium—apart, of course, from industrial occupation and habits—could be employed for the reclamation of all that is reclaimable in criminal lives than a judiciously stocked prison library, in which the moral-teaching and wrong-punishing description of novel should be largely represented— where truth and honesty are made to triumph over their opposite vices, and the precepts and duties of religious, moral, and industrial citizenship are held up as the standard of social obligations, and the surest guarantees of worldly happiness and prosperity. Direct Scripture or moral teaching, either through religious works or the labours of prison chaplains, is all but useless with criminals, and, as a method, is as unpopular in the work of obtaining reformatory results as direct taxation would be to the grumbling citizen, if all he really does pay had to be parted with in a painfully objective manner But let a method of indirect teaching be resorted to, no matter how moral the ideas or religious the lessons taught, if but accompanied with narrative, interesting delineations of character, and something approaching to a plot, and every sentiment and every line will be read and talked over. In fact it is only what prisoners read between labour hours in prison that can come between themselves and their thoughts of crime past, and reveries of criminal deeds to come; and too much cannot be done in the way of supplying healthy and acceptable mental food to be placed in opposition to the criminal broodings of morally perverted minds. For work of this kind too much praise cannot be bestowed upon the serial publications issued by Cassell and Company, Messrs. Chambers of Edinburgh, and a few others of a more decidedly religious tone, such as the *Leisure Hour, Sunday at Home, Good Words, The Lamp,* &c

In respect to these latter mediums of moral instruction, it is a pity that sectarianism is so often displayed in their pages that the Catholic chaplains of convict prisons interdict their delivery to Catholic prisoners. This is unfortunate, as the only Catholic serial publication found in a convict prison library, namely, *The Lamp,* is not of itself adequate to the performance of the good offices fulfilled for Protestant prisoners by the numerous journals which they are privileged to read. No more effective reformer ever entered the gates of a prison than *Cassell's Family Magazine,* with its select stories, its charming pictures of *home life,* its lessons upon most subjects that belong to the sphere of the intelligent artisan class of society, and its instructive, moral, cheerful, and piquant *tout ensemble.* Nor, in alluding to the importance of instilling pure thoughts and clean ideas into morally diseased minds, should *Chambers's Journal* and *Papers for the People* be omitted Apart from the moral good which these three last periodicals have undoubtedly achieved among those convicts who have been made familiar with them in prison, I owe them a debt of gratitude myself for the many pleasant hours which they have been the chief means of enabling me to pass where otherwise the very idea of pleasure was but a mockery and a pain.

The next kind of favourite prison literature is biography, in which department there is also ample scope for the inculcation of doctrines and precepts that would be certain of rejection if offered in the form of direct religious teaching. Half a prison library might be stocked with biographies of self-made and remarkable men, the struggles and achievements of whose lives would constitute the best class of reading that could be offered to those who, above everything else, stand in need of instruction by example.

With the exception of poetry and history, the remaining branches of English literature represented in a prison library are not very much patronised by convicts, the general demand upon the schoolmaster being for the lighter kind of reading, and of this in the order in which I have specified it

I have talked with a number of professional thieves

who had acquired a knowledge of French somewhere, and who were more or less familiar with the French poets and most celebrated writers in that language, while possessing a very fair proficiency in the literature of their own country. Such men had probably mastered French while in companionship with French thieves in prison, French grammars for the use of convicts who are Frenchmen being among the educational books allowed to prisoners   These helps, and the presence of numbers of Frenchmen in nearly every convict establishment, who would, of course, give and take in the way of linguistic instruction, is another explanation. I was one day in exercising file with a "flash" or swell young pickpocket who had succeeded in picking up a smattering of French, of which he was very vain Upon the termination of his sentence he was resolved upon leaving "this blooming stupid land of England and going to reside in France."

"What to do ?" I was curious enough to ask.

"Why, to do the aristocrat," was his reply.   "Little Jemmy S——, who is in the tailors' party, and myself are to go together, and represent ourselves as two English lords"

"Well, and how do you intend to work the oracle ?" I inquired

"Supposing," he answered, "one of us to succeed

in obtaining an introduction to a very swell family, we
could easily bone their jewellery and other valuable
swag. Jemmy, who is reckoned a first-class hand at
almost everything, would get up in the night-time, do
the place, and let it be supposed that the house was
rifled by French thieves"

"But how would you get the swag removed?"

"Oh! as to that," he replied, "why, I would be
under the window with a wheelbarrow, and secure all
the swag in that way."

A very nice position for a pair of English lords!

The Religion of Convicts.—There is nothing touching
the prison welfare of a convict so carefully looked
to by the prison authorities as his religion. The portion of the prison rules which deals with that part
of a prisoner's treatment is so carefully read over
to him, and so explained, that it is impossible for a
follower of one particular creed to find himself classed
as a member of any other, or compelled to be present
at a religious service which he has not previously
consented to attend. This, of course, is as it ought to
be; yet one who should infer from it that all the
members of convict Protestant or Catholic congrega-
tions were respectively all Protestants and Catholics
would fall into a good-sized error. With the exception
of non-Cockney Irish Catholics and Scotch Presby-

terians, the particular religion of an habitual jail-bird
is a matter of very little concern to himself, and
is made a secondary consideration to less worthy
motives

If a London thief, professing Protestantism, should
have a pal undergoing a term of penal servitude who
was a Catholic, he would, to a certainty, class himself
as a member of the latter faith after being sentenced,
in hopes of falling in with his old chum somewhere
and at some period during the lagging; while a similar
object would guide the religious profession of a London
Catholic "gunn" if the case were reversed.

In addition to this motive in the matter of choosing
a religion, the point is also determined by the particular
faith which was professed in a previous imprisonment,
should the prisoner be a re-convicted prisoner, as this
class of criminal very rarely appears under the same
religious banner again, unless compelled by the number
of his convictions, and the scarcity of creeds, to fall
back upon an old faith

There was one of this class in Dartmoor, named
Barmy Harrison, who had gone through three laggings
in that prison, each in connection with a separate religion. He was first a Jew, next a Protestant, and then
a Catholic, and upon my asking him one day how he
would shift when convicted again (as convicted he

would be, if there was anything in London to be stolen
for the sake of theft), he answered that he would put
himself down as a follower of Mohammed. Owing to
the Catholic chaplain prohibiting nearly all the serial
journals included in the prison library (to which I have
already alluded) from circulation among Catholic prisoners, numbers of the latter not only put themselves down
as Protestants when re-convicted, but demand that they
be permitted to change during the imprisonment upon
that account alone   As all parties concerned—Protestant and Catholic chaplains—consent in most instances
to this arrangement, the desired religious transfer is
made, and the "conscience" of the convert is quieted.
Reasons often occur on the other side, also, which
induce some who are Protestants to go over to the
side of Rome for the remainder of the sentence, and, of
course, to profess neither faith for an hour after the
sentence shall expire.

The Scotch Presbyterian, however, will never turn
Catholic, no matter how often he is lagged, or what the
inducement may be that would turn the thoughts of
other Protestants in that direction, and on their part
the same may be said in reference to "conversion" of
nearly all Irish Catholic prisoners, the afore-mentioned
Cockney Irish excepted. It would be a mistake, however, to infer from this religious "consistency" that

those who show such evidence of an allegiance to one faith are therefore considerably less inclined to the commission of crime than the indifferent. It is by no means the least of the many saddening reflections which a prison experience engenders, that religion in prison is in nine cases out of ten put on either for dishonest purposes, or assumed in the no less reprehensible game of hypocrisy.

LECTURE XX.

PRISON ANECDOTES.

In the Wrong Hotel—Negative Definition of a Gentleman—
Unappreciated Merit—Cause for an English Revolution—
How an Irish Republic lost an English Advocate.

In *the Wrong Hotel*—The hour of bed-time in Newgate—six o'clock—did not invite a sudden falling off
into an obliviousness of a sentence of fifteen years
When one is but twenty-three years of age and has
only a two months' experience of the loss of liberty and
one day of actual penal servitude, all that such a fate
includes at that period of life, was not easy to drown
in slumber at such an hour. In addition to this source
of wakefulness, the thousand and one noises of London
that pierce the walls of Newgate would make sleep
impossible on the first night after all hope of liberty
had been crushed out of the heart by a terrible sentence,
at least until the small hours of morning should silence

the disturbing cries. The hour of midnight had just
struck from the belfries of all the churches in the
vicinity, St. Paul's toning down the jingling concert
with its thick mellow strokes; while the rich bass of
Big Ben came lumbering up the Thames and across
the City with its melancholy chimes of the "Old
Hundredth," as if it were anxious to sing all other
noises to silence and repose, when the signal-bell in
the cell next to mine sent its sharp warning through
the whole corridor, as if it, too, had been set in motion
through a sympathy with the hundred bells that had
just died out on the midnight air. After a few minutes'
silence the signal was again struck, accompanied, this
time, by some indistinct muttering, as if the person
who had pulled it was in bad humour with whatever
necessity awoke him from slumber. Anon the slow
tread of the night guard passed by my door, and,
pausing at that of the disturber, I heard a sharp
voice say, "Well, what is it?" The reply was so in-
audible that I failed to catch any portion of it but the
word "want," and from the answer which it elicited
from the guard I guessed that some unusual request
had been made by my next-door neighbour. "Oh! is
that all? You have made a slight mistake, my man,
and come to the wrong place. Go to bed." And after
delivering himself of this piece of advice, the guard
repassed my door, and all was silent for a couple of

minutes. Bang! goes the signal-bell again; and evoking no response, my neighbour, who had now recovered his voice, shouted, loud enough to be heard all over the prison, "Waiter! I say, waiter!" No reply, of course. Loud muttering by the voice, as if he was expressing in anything but polite language his appreciation of the party for whom he was calling, when—bang! goes the signal again, while the impassioned individual followed it up with, "Waiter, I tell you I can't find the matches! I want a light and a glass of brandy-and-water!" A titter of half-suppressed laughter from the adjoining cells told me that my neighbour had enlarged his audience by his demands, when the signal was struck once more. No response. The voice, manifestly suffering from feelings of evident disgust, shouted, "Is there no use in my ringing or shouting—Waiter?" No reply. The voice again, this time as if moralising with himself, "Well, I have been in a good many hotels in my time in London and elsewhere, but such a d——d place as this is I never put up in before. Waiter!" thundered at the cell door, somewhere near where the keyhole should be. No response. The voice, in a towering rage, and as if intended to penetrate to that supposed region where mine host would be likely to hear it—"Bring me my bill! I won't stop another hour in this d——d place!" A shout of laughter from the whole corridor at this threat to dispatronise the "hotel" Newgate brought the guard instanter again to the scene of the disturbance, and after a few words from him as to the "slight mistake" into which my neighbour had fallen, the place resumed its former silence, the guard muttering in passing my door, "A fit of the blues."

A Negative Definition of a Gentleman—One of the most unpopular among the prisoners in Dartmoor during his stay in that prison was an individual who passed himself off as a Major-general H——, and to whom I have already alluded in some of my remarks upon aristocratic impostors. He was a man of very commanding presence, and had, probably, been a private in the Guards ere commencing his swindling career. But if his military air, assumed rank, and lofty demeanour had enabled him to pass himself off upon portions of the outside public as somebody in particular, they failed to gain him anything from the thievocracy of Dartmoor save a constant warfare of petty annoyance. This he, to some extent, merited at their hands from his contemptuous behaviour towards any of them who chanced to get into the same exercising file along with him, and his constant boast that he was no thief, but a "gentleman." His claim to the latter distinction was, of course, as much ridiculed as his assumed military rank, and both of these pretensions were the means of keeping him in hot water with the rest of the prisoners with whom he was associated. One of those whom he had one day snubbed for venturing to speak to him, put to me the following question a few days afterwards, in reference to the "general" and himself.— "Look here, you answer me this: Whether is a bloke who is a pickpocket, and honest enough to admit it, or a fellow who has been a swell swindler and has been lagged for bigamy, but tries to pass himself off as a gentleman, the biggest scoundrel?"

I felt bound to decide against the latter, as he was guilty of two species of scoundrelism to the former's one; whereupon my interrogator exclaimed— "I thought so, and the next time the 'general' snubs me, I'll give him a punch on the blooming nose."

The "general's" last offence, I may here remark, was a case of heartless bigamy. He had succeeded in introducing himself to a young lady in London who possessed a small fortune of 600*l.*, to obtain which he committed this crime; and being tried and convicted received five years' penal servitude This fact, added to his conduct towards those who had been guilty of less infamy than had been brought home to himself subjected him to all the persecution which could be given without attracting the attention of the warders; while no one could be induced to sympathise with him owing to his repellent behaviour and ridiculous assumptions. There was one exception, however, to this, in the conduct of a young Irish lad, named Mulligan, whom the "general" had patronised, ostensibly because he was not a thief—Mulligan having been sentenced, as expressed by himself, "for flooring a policeman with a poker" The "general" condescended to walk and talk with Mulligan, while Mulligan would threaten to box whoever should cast a suspicion upon his patron's claims to a gentleman's position in outside society. "I tell ye he *is* a gintleman," Mulligan would say. "Don't I know a gintleman from a thief and robber; and didn't he tell me that his house has railin's round it! What do the likes of ye know about a gintleman!" After a time the true nature of his partiality for Mulligan began to show itself, as the latter was observed to save most of his bread; and the rumour went around that Mulligan was "slinging toke" (giving his bread) to the "general." This only tended to increase the unpopularity of the latter when it was known he was accepting the poor lad's loaves while on light-labour rations, and the whole of No. 2 prison, where the parties were located, became a "razor" upon him for· this fresh proof of his meanness. Nothing, however, would make the slightest impression upon Mulligan's faith in the respectability of the man who was growing fat upon his generosity, until the object of it overdid his part one day, and henceforth placed Mulligan in the ranks of his enemies. The "general" and his inseparable companion had just commenced exercising one fine frosty morning, such a morning as would give any healthy person a keen appetite, when the following dialogue was overheard between them :

General. "Now, Mulligan, I am more and more delighted with your society every day, as I find you are a manly and intelligent little fellow; and let me see, now, if you can't bring me out your pudding to-morrow."

Mulligan (indignantly). "Now luk here, gineral, this is comin id too much altogether ! When all the prison was agin you and said you was an imposthor, I tuk your part, and said you were a gintleman ; but now I find out you are nothin' of the sort; for a thrue gintleman would never take a man's bread to-day, and thin ask him for his puddin' to-morrow ! I tuk pity on you because you were a big man, but as I find you are no gintleman, don't expect bread or puddin' from me any more."

Unappreciated Merit —One of the labour gangs to which I was for some time attached after my arrival in Dartmoor was made up of eight prisoners—six London pickpockets, a Yorkshire thief known as Old Peter, and myself. The work at which we were employed offered considerable latitude for talk, on which privilege the Cockney hooks were only too prone to seize, in order to recount to each other the thieving exploits and police adventures in which they had figured during their respective careers. The six Londoners would always so arrange their work as to remain, if possible, within talking distance of each other, while completely ignoring the presence of Old Peter and myself. This arrangement was by no means as agreeable to Peter as it was to me, for he was forced thereby to a labour association with one who was altogether outside the profession, being thus deprived of all the pleasure which the professional company of six seemed to enjoy in congenial society. Often have I been amused at seeing Old Peter hovering near the charmed circle, as a schoolboy would cling to a wall inside of which a game of football was being played, from any participation in which he would be rigorously excluded by the selfish gamesters; and I could easily fancy the old fellow lamenting the unlucky fate which had fixed his birthplace in Yorkshire instead of in London. Something more than usually piquant was being talked over one day by the privileged six that threw them into occasional fits of merriment, and which put Old Peter into a correspondingly depressed mood through being a witness of what he had not the gratification of participating in. It was more than flesh and blood could stand to be thus "so near and yet so far" from the object of one's desire, so Old Peter, mustering up fresh resolution, took his shovel and walked to the place where the six were working and chatting, and commenced to dig and listen. A costermonger intruding into a Belgravia drawing-room could not be more promptly expelled than was poor Peter, who was indignantly asked "What did the old gowk want there?" Thus unfeelingly repelled, Peter walked slowly back to where I was standing, a witness of his humiliation, and, leaning upon his shovel as if in the agony of disgrace, he muttered, "I'm a gowk! Ov coorse I'm nowt, becose I donno cum fro Lunnon! Bud I'll tell thee wod" (fiercely addressing me), "I stowl watches forty yer sin—long afore them chaps wer born! Bud," (continued he sorrowfully, while resuming his work near me), "that's nowt, becose—I dunno cum fro Lunnon!" I have often thought that Old Peter's was as cruel an instance of unappreciated merit as any that came under my observation while studying the caste of crime.

Cause for an English Revolution.—The addition of a "new chum" to the wards of any convict prison is a matter of excitement to the prisoners therein located until it becomes known who he is, where he has come from, and for what particular offence he has been introduced to penal society. If information on these points be not at once obtainable, the new-comer is

described to be just what his particular neighbours
desire him to be   A little extra officiousness on the
part of the Millbank warders having surrounded my
entrance into that establishment, it became somewhat
difficult for the inquisitive prisoners to learn what
would satisfy their curiosity in my regard. For a
couple of days after my "reception" I was constantly
being interrogated as to where I had been "collared,"
what I had "boned," and where I had done my "last
bit" These questions would be addressed to me after
meal times while the warders would be absent from
the wards—a time when loud whispering could be
carried on through the curious inspection holes which
formed a peculiar feature in the architecture of the
Millbank cells

On the second evening in my new lodgings I went
to the spy hole, after hearing the turnkey lock the
ward gate and descend the stairs to his tea. Skilly
had just been served out to the thirty inhabitants of
that particular ward, and a furious application of
wooden spoons to the bottoms of empty cans spoke
eloquently of the appetites of my new associates.
After the noise had subsided

A voice exclaimed—"I say, Bill, were you ever
choked off with such blooming thin skilly in all
your lagging?"

Bill, from a cell higher up the ward—"The blooming

guv'nor fattens his pigs with the meal and only allows one ounce for a pint "

Another voice—" I say, pals, who is the new chum in No. 7 " (my cell) " who won't mag ? " (talk).

First voice—"He has done a tenner in Gib for a burst in the city, and is sent back on his ticket "

A fourth voice—" Get along, you duffer ! He has only one duke " (arm), " and the orderly told me to-day that he has got fifteen stretch for being a Fenian."

Bill's chum, sympathetically—" Poor fellow ! I knew a lot a Fenians when I was a doin' my last bit in Woking. They were rare chums for slinging toke !' (giving away bread)

After which, the same voice, by way of encouragement—" It's time there was a blooming revolution in England when a bloke like me gets seven stretch for boning a coat, and gets skilly like this to live upon !"

I immediately collapsed.

How an Irish Republic lost an English Advocate.—I was accosted while at exercise one morning in the stone-breaking party in Dartmoor by an old white-headed man, speaking a broad, north-country dialect, with a—" Tha art a polytikle prisoner, I believe ? " I replied that such was the nature of the charge that had been made against me. " So am I, and I am veria weel pleased as we con toke together," was the rejoinder of my new acquaintance. I was soon placed in possession of the old man's history, and was agreeably surprised to find behind a strong provincialism of speech and manner an intelligence and a knowledge of political history far beyond what is usually found among English working men. Old D——s had been a Chartist in '48, and held to his principles in every political contest that had occurred in his native town down to one of an unusually bitter character which took place at the general election of '68, when he was concerned in an election riot in which some property was destroyed, was arrested, tried, and sentenced to five years' penal servitud This piece of injustice, as he termed it, soured the old man's feelings against those who had the administration of English law in their hands, and made him cling all the more tenaciously to the principles he had imbibed from the *Northern Star* and Chartist leaders in the stormy epoch of '48. He was the first intelligent Englishman I had met with who had read Irish history in order to view the Anglo-Irish question from both sides, and who had the liberality to admit and declare that his country had never a valid title to hold Ireland in unwilling political subjection. Whatever other claim to its possession might be put forward by Englishmen, he would declare, could not stand the test of common sense or justice in the face of England's manifest failure to govern the people of Ireland in a manner that was beneficial to their social welfare, or conducive to the peace and general good of the two countries. He did not believe in that kind of imperial prestige which was acquired at the expense of justice, and which was built upon a robbed and ruined India or a pauperised and disaffected Ireland Real imperial greatness consisted in an enfranchised people, free trade in the broadest acceptation of the term, just laws and their impartial administration, free public education, and the eradicating of poverty by the readjustment of the land laws, so as to distribute the land as much as possible. He was ashamed of the crimes that had been perpetrated in the name of England upon the people of Ireland, and for his part he would sanction a political separation of the two countries to-morrow, and wish prosperity and happiness to an Irish Republic!

I could not help expressing my surprise to find an intelligent Englishman holding such extremely liberal views upon England's rule of Ireland, and I ventured to say that very few more advocates of separation would be found among his countrymen. "My dear sir," he answered, "you mistake ignorance for prejudice when you take it for granted that all Englishmen are dead opposed to an independent Ireland. Let them inquire into the way in which that unfortunate country has been ruled by our kings and parliaments, in the name of Englishmen, and they will arrive at the conclusion which has been forced upon me by the study of Irish history. What guide have they to the formation of a just and impartial opinion in those of our English historians who have written upon the connection of the two countries? None whatever. Give them your side of the question, and rely upon it that justice will be done Englishmen are not afraid to do right when they once learn that they have been ignorantly in the wrong" Such, divested of their northern dialect, were the opinions which old D——s invariably put forward as expressive of his views upon the vexed subject of his country's government of Ireland, and I had no reason whatever to suspect them to be anything else but the just and honest convictions of a fair-minded, inquiring Englishman. The old man delighted in re-counting his conversations with Fergus O'Connor, who was extremely popular in mid-Yorkshire, and was fond of boasting that he had once shaken hands with O'Connell. He could recite the whole of Robert Emmet's speech from the dock, and I was agreeably surprised to hear him declare that the likeness of this, the purest type of Irish political martyr, could be found in hundreds of farm-houses throughout what D——s was pleased to call "democratic Yorkshire"

These facts, joined to the old man's extensive

reading and amount of general information, rendered him a very interesting and acceptable companion under the circumstances, and I always looked forward to a half hour's exercise in his company with a great deal of pleasure. Unfortunately for his peace of mind he was possessed of two of the worst attributes that a man could bring with him into prison and the society of thieves—a bad temper, and a constant habit of boasting that he was an honest man. The first of these incumbrances involved poor D——s in constant trivial breaches of the prison rules, for which he had, of course, to suffer the prescribed penalty; while the other invited a far more unbearable species of annoyance from the thievocracy. To get along well with the latter in prison it is not at all necessary that a non-professional should either advocate or condone the calling of a burglar or pickpocket, or even refrain from passing sentence upon thieving in general. But to expect a thief who is undergoing the same punishment as his critic, and who is placed upon an equal footing with him in regard to law and prison discipline, to listen patiently and submit to a comparison between honesty and dishonesty as represented by two men in convict dress, would be as ridiculous as to expect a fishwoman having herrings of a questionable freshness to be silent while another would be lauding apparently similar goods at the expense of her own.

Old D——s had never viewed the character of his prison associates in this light, but thought it a duty due to his own moral integrity to draw a contrast between that and its obliquity in others whenever he would be placed in exercising file with any pickpocket, and as a natural consequence was disliked and persecuted by most of those with whom he was in daily contact

Our party was employed in stone-breaking one beautiful June morning, in a portion of the prison-yard where we could command a pleasing view of the Devonshire hills as they roll away from Dartmoor in the direction of Exeter.   D——s and I, while cracking our granite, were, endeavouring to recall some portion of Yorkshire scenery that would favourably compare with what was stretched before us, clothed in the bright verdure of the season, and laughing under the genial influence of the summer's sun.   From scenery to politics, and from Dartmoor to Ireland, were easy conversational transitions under the circumstances, and D——s waxed more than ever indignantly eloquent and vehemently just at the expense of his country's past misdeeds and present culpability in reference to its treatment of " the sister country."   " Justice must be done though the heavens should fall.   The time was fast approaching when *the people* of England would be enlightened enough, and the franchise extended enough, to enable them to think and act for themselves, and to make some atonement for the crimes of the past by allowing the Irish to select what form of government might best conform to their national feelings and social requirements. The only prejudice that an educated English nation would probably cling to the longest was that against the creed of the Irish people; but though he (D——s) was opposed to all priestcraft, the religion of a people was their own concern, and should not weigh against the rendering of political justice to them. Macaulay was censurable for the bitterness with which he assailed both the Irish and their national faith; but his teaching would have little effect upon the judgment of the rising generation of his country-men, who would be guided by pure reason and a love of justice in their dealings with Ireland," &c., &c. Thus did the old man hold out upon the future policy of England, and the bright destiny in store for the land of Fergus O'Connor and Emmet, which would follow from the awakening sense of right and duty of the new England that popular education was now develop-ing so rapidly. But alas! for the Isle of Destiny, and the realisation of D——s' dream of an Irish Republic established by English love of justice! The evil genius of Ireland, that has so often marred the efforts that might deliver her, was again at hand, to dash the hopes and prospects of her liberty to earth once more. This

evil genius has appeared under divers circumstances
and forms throughout the long and dark period of
seven centuries. At one time it is dissension among
Irish chieftains; at another it is want of true patriotic
courage in the leaders of an armed volunteer force in
face of a helpless alien garrison; next it is a storm
that scatters a fleet in Bantry Bay, then the deadly
blight of treason blasting the hopes of the brave when
thinking of victory and freedom, and in the instance
I am now relating this evil genius had clothed itself in
the personality of a London pickpocket, by name
" Mick the Spaniard" Unfortunately for D——s'
English-made Irish Republic this wretch was not from
the land of El Caballero della Trieste Figuera, but was
supposed from his abbreviated Christian name to hail
from quite another part of the world, while in reality
he was a born Cockney, who was known among his
professional associates by the above double misnomer
for some reason or other of which history must remain
ignorant He is the same individual who "chucked the
dummy," as related in a former lecture, and was, of all
the hooks I ever met in prison, the very incarnation
of theft and mischief During the foregoing conversations between old D——s and myself, "the Spaniard"
occupied the seat on my left, and was an eager listener
to all that was said upon Anglo-Irish politics; but
never a word said he. D——s and he had encountered

each other upon more than one occasion, when the old subject of honesty *versus* thieving was thrashed out; "Mick," of course, not only calling the old man's profession of that virtue into question, but affirming that no such article was to be found anywhere in society, and that thieving was man's natural vocation. Of all the enemies which D——s' defence of honesty had made him among the pickpockets of Dartmoor, "Mick" was the most malignant; and the only barrier between them upon this momentous occasion was the seat occupied by myself.

In the midst of one of D——s' narratives of Chartist days, I was suddenly called upon by the warder, in company with a few other members of the party, to do some work at the other extremity of the prison yard, which would occupy about an hour in its performance, and, to my regret, neither D——s nor "Mick" were included in the sub-party, as I was not without fears that the old man would fare badly in close quarters with such a character as now sat beside him. On my return from the temporary occupation just referred to, the first object which attracted my attention was a prodigious heap of broken stones in front of old D——s, while his hammer was scattering splinters of granite in every direction, indicating the presence of some unusual excitement as being responsible for this extraordinary manual exertion. On resuming my place between

" Mick" and D——s, I observed the tears rolling down the old man's cheeks, and I guessed at once that an encounter had taken place, in which the young ruffian had grievously hurt the feelings of his companion. When upon the point of inquiring what had happened, I was interrupted by old D——s (who had apparently taken no notice of my return) muttering audibly, while his hammer was still going as if driven by steam, " I war olus towd so, bud couldn't believe id. Neea, I foind id's bud too thru ! Macaulay is reet, afther all they are nowt bud a people as is fit fur priestcraft or slavery !" " Why, D——s," I broke in, " what is the matter ?" " I've stud up for 'em," he continued, without deigning to notice my question, " monny a hundred toimes against my own countryfolk ; bud I shall never do so again—never ! They are nod desarving on't." " Oh, come, D——s, old fellow, what *has* caused all this excitement ?" I again asked. " Id's this !" he fiercely retorted ; " I shall never oppen me meeath again fur th' Irish people. They're being treated just as they desarve, and I shall not only never advocate a separation fra England ony moor, bud I'll tek up arms, if needs be, to prevent it ! Owd Oliver's gred mistake ware in nod driving 'em all into t'sea" " But what has *caused* all this, D——s ?" I asked again " *Why, that red-yeded Irish thief theere*" (pointing to " Mick ") " *has spit i' me face !*" he hurled out with increased vehemence, and then resumed his hostile muttering against the hapless people from whom some one, in an evil hour, had borrowed part of a nickname for the cause of the old man's wrath. Upon demanding an explanation from " Mick," that gentleman coolly informed me that he had attempted to occupy my seat while I was away, whereupon D——s interfered, saying that he did not want any Irish thief near him, " and as I would be reported if I gave him a punch in the nose, I spit in his face, as I am not going to stand cheek from an old gowk of a Yorkshire swine like him," was the reply of the evil genius who had caused an Irish Republic to lose an enthusiastic English advocate

I do not desire you to believe that *all* Englishmen who call themselves Radicals and friends of Ireland have sympathies and convictions towards that unfortunate country as easily uprooted as those of old D——s No—not all

PART II.

SOCIAL EVILS AND SUGGESTED REMEDIES.

IN the preceding twenty lectures we have travelled over the first portion of our task. In many respects it has not been an agreeable one, I admit. The dark side of human nature is neither an interesting nor a consolatory study. So fond are we of admiring the good and the beautiful in humanity, that we are only too prone to ignore the existence of its bad and repulsive features until they obtrude themselves upon us in a manner that is anything but complimentary to our self-complacent civilisation. Crimes, criminals, and prisons are phases of our social life which few people, beyond judges, police officials, and jailers, care to trouble their minds about. This is all the worse for the society which engenders such indifference, for the more this criminal skeleton in the cupboard of our modern civilisation is revealed in all its reproaching realism, the sooner will such means be discovered as will either reduce its hideous proportions or succeed in circumscribing its opportunities for evil.

We have, so far, dealt with numerous kinds of crime,

and have photographed various types of criminal; but, as yet, we have done no more than hint at such remedies as we shall be expected to propose in the task of minimising criminal propensities and pursuits in the individual, and increasing the methods of deterrency in the state.

I might now attempt to outline these remedies, but before doing so it may be well to deal more specifically with the subject of penal servitude, or the punishment which the rulers of English society inflict upon those who war against their laws   This can best be done by my giving you a short summary of this system, and then offering such comments and suggestions thereon as appear to me to be just, necessary, and feasible

LECTURE XXI.

THE PUNISHMENT OF PENAL SERVITUDE.

Brief description of Penal Servitude by Lord Kimberley's Royal Commission—Disciplinary Classification of Convicts—Evils of and Remedies for Present System—"Solitary" in its Relation to Deterrency — Penal Colonies — Re-Convicted Criminals—Circumstantial Evidence at Fault—Non-Discriminating Discipline—Anomaly in Sentences—Summary of Penal Servitude

THE following brief description of penal servitude is taken from the Report by the Penal Servitude Acts Commission, 1879 (vol. 1 pages 14-19) ·—

"Excepting the convicts at large on license, and a limited number in Western Australia (the diminishing remnant of the abandoned system of transportation) the male convicts of Great Britain are confined in the prisons of Borstal, Brixton, Chatham (with its subsidiary establishment at Chattenden), Dartmoor, Millbank, Parkhurst, Pentonville, Portland, Portsmouth,

Woking, and Wormwood Scrubs. At Millbank and Pentonville convicts undergo a period of separate confinement, and at the other prisons, which are termed 'public works prisons,' they work in association. The new prison still constructing at Wormwood Scrubs, though now used as a public works prison, is intended when completed to replace Millbank (which is to be discontinued) as a prison for the detention of male and female convicts in separate confinement.

" A sentence to penal servitude includes, as regards the male convicts of Great Britain, three stages—(1) a period of strict separate confinement, (2) a period on public works, (3) a period on license, if remission of any portion of the sentence be earned.

"In accordance with the opinion of the Commission of 1863, the first stage, which is passed at Millbank or Pentonville, extends in all cases over a term of nine months. In this stage convicts work, sleep, and have their meals each in his own cell. They are in the presence of each other in the daily exercise (for one hour a day) and the daily attendance at chapel, but they are then in silent association. The visits to the cells by the governor, the medical officer, the chaplain, and subordinate officers of the prison alone break the silence and solitude of their lives. The convicts are principally employed in tailoring, hammock and bag making, shoe-making, mat-making, weaving, and oakum-picking.

Ignorant or imperfectly educated convicts receive instruction once or twice a week in reading, writing,
and arithmetic, and their progress is tested by half-
yearly examinations.   All, moreover, are supplied with
religious and educational books, and with a limited
number of works of general literature, which are called
'library books.'

"After the first nine months convicts are removed
to a public works prison, and there enter upon the
second and longest stage of penal discipline. Excepting some invalid and aged convicts at Parkhurst and
Woking, who live entirely in association, convicts on
public works sleep and have their meals in separate
cells, but labour in association; all communication,
however, being prohibited beyond what is indispensable for their work.

"The distribution of employments is regulated in
part by the requirements of the service, and in part
by the physical capacities, skill, and conduct of the
prisoners   Building and engineering for the convict
service are carried on at all the prisons, and large works,
including excavations, brick-making, and every branch
of building are executing by convict labour for the
Admiralty or the War Office, or for both those departments, at Borstal, Chatham, Portland, and Portsmouth
Extensive reclamation of moorland is conducted at
Dartmoor, and farming supplies a suitable occupation

for prisoners who are unequal to the severest kinds of labour in the open air   The same occupation is pursued at Parkhurst and Woking, to which prisons invalid, and weak-minded convicts are sent.   Various trades, such as tailoring, shoe-making, carpentering, and blacksmiths' work, are also carried on in all the prisons, and the superior attractiveness of such kinds of labour furnishes an incentive to good conduct.

"Convicts on public works attend chapel daily. But the practice, to which the Commission of 1863 took exception, of giving convicts schooling in hours that would otherwise be devoted to labour, has been discontinued, and the schooling now takes place in the evening after working hours. The time, therefore, devoted to instruction, and especially in the summer months, is less in the public works prisons than during the period of separate confinement. The arrangements with respect to the supply of books to prisoners are similar in both these stages of penal servitude

"Convicts engaged in indoor employments are allowed daily a period of exercise (usually about an hour), and all are allowed, according to their class, one or more periods of exercise on Sundays. Formerly they took this exercise in groups of twos or threes, but recently the practice of exercise in single file has been introduced as regards male convicts.

"Under the present system of classification, which

was adopted in 1864, there are five classes in ascending scale, viz., the probation, the third, the second, the first, and the special classes Promotion from a lower to a higher class is gained by good conduct and industry; subject, however, to the conditions that the minimum period passed in each of the probation, the third, and the second classes, must be one year; that no convict can be admitted into the first class until he can read or write, unless exemption from this condition be granted by a director; and that the special class cannot be entered without exemplary conduct in the first class, and until within twelve months of discharge from prison. Each class has its own distinctive marks of dress; and promotion in class brings an increase of privileges as regards frequency of communication with friends by letters and by visits, in the amount of exercise on Sundays, and in the rate of gratuity which may be earned. With slight exceptions affecting the second, first, and special classes, all dietary privileges have been abolished since 1864.

"The regulations now in force as to marks and gratuities date from the same year. The Commission of 1863 condemned the then existing system of marks as needlessly complicated, and as having the fault of assuming that the remission would be granted unless it were forfeited in whole or part as a penalty, instead of holding it out as a reward to be earned by good conduct and industry. They were of opinion that credit should not be given for general good conduct, as well as for industry, good conduct in prison (apart from industry) being merely abstinence from misconduct. They also thought that convicts should not be able to earn marks in separate confinement, and they advocated the adoption of such a system as would provide a daily record of each prisoner's industry

"These requirements of the Commission have been met. No marks can now be earned by good conduct alone, nor apart from good conduct can they be earned by industry. Forfeiture of marks, involving prolonged detention in a lower class or curtailment of the period on license, or both these penalties, at the discretion of the director or governor by whom the convict's offence is judged, is the most common of prison punishments. No marks can be earned during separate confinement, but marks may be prospectively forfeited by misconduct during that period.

"By the existing scale eight marks per diem are allowed for steady hard labour and the full performance of the allotted task, seven marks for a less degree of industry, and six for a fair but moderate day's work. No remission being granted in the period of separate confinement, a convict on public works daily obtaining eight marks earns the maximum amount of remission, viz , one-fourth of so much of the term of his sentence as is spent on public works; while the convict who never obtains more than six marks per diem earns no remission, and therefore serves the entire term of his sentence in prison Convicts in the light labour classes are credited with only six or seven marks per diem, according to their character and industry, unless the labour be regarded as skilled labour, in which case full marks may be earned Convicts in hospital are not credited with more than six marks per diem, except by special permission of a director. On Sundays marks are granted for conduct alone at the rate at which the prisoner has earned them during the working days of the week The marks are daily awarded and recorded by the warders in charge of the working parties, and the governors and deputy-governors of the prisons are enjoined to see that this duty is fairly and efficiently performed Every convict is supplied with a card, which records the number of marks and the amount of gratuity that he may have gained or lost in each quarter.

"The Commission of 1863 disapproved the large gratuities then given to convicts, as having the effect of rendering penal servitude in some rare cases an object of desire rather than of apprehension, and as having the further serious fault of enabling those whose sentences were the longest, and whose crimes were therefore pre-

sumably the gravest, to earn the largest sums of money.
These evils were remedied by the changes made in
1864. The amount of gratuity which may now be
earned is dependent upon the prisoner's class. But
convicts in the first class cannot earn a larger gratuity
than 3*l*, and those who reach the special class and
place themselves under a Prisoners' Aid Society may
earn an extra gratuity of 3*l*, making in all 6*l* An
instalment of the gratuity earned is paid to the prisoner
at the time of his discharge, and the residue is subsequently remitted to him through the agency of the
police of the district where he has gone to reside, or
of a Prisoners' Aid Society if he has chosen to accept
their assistance. To convicts whose conduct has been
bad and who have earned no gratuity a sum of 10*s*.
is usually given on discharge."

The foregoing statement is but a bare and colour-
less description of penal servitude, as it has presented
itself to the members of a Royal Commission, from
the standpoint of an official inquiry. You will readily
admit that it must necessarily assume quite another
complexion when considered from the point of view of
a many years' actual experience of its punishment It
is from this "fulness of knowledge" I shall speak of
it in the present lecture. But I may at once remark
that it is not my intention to harrow your feelings with

a tale of personal suffering Such a narrative does not come within the scope of these lectures, and in any case it would be doubly painful to obtrude one's own bitter experiences when criticising defective systems and searching out the best remedies for general social evils.

(The following lecture was mostly contributed as a paper to the *Contemporary Review* for August 1883, and is inserted here by the kind permission of the editor. It was originally mainly copied from my Portland notes.)

I propose in this lecture to point out such defects in this system as appear susceptible of amendment, and to offer a few suggestions on the correlative subject of criminal reformation such as my experience of convict life and observation of criminal character enable me to make. I do not intend to enter into an examination of the management of convict prisons, as my immediate object is to discuss the more important topic of the penalties awarded to criminals, and the extent to which their infliction deters from the commission of crime, or reforms from evil habits.

Classification of Convicts.—How far the recommendations that were made in the Report of the recent Commission which was appointed to investigate the

working of the Penal Servitude Acts, have been carried
out by the directors of convict prisons, is not easy
for the public to fully ascertain   The general election
of 1880 and the subsequent absorbing events have
put the punishment of criminals and the management
of convict prisons in the background of public questions ; and prison officials are not over-communicative
when popular interest is not excited in connection with
their department of the Civil Service. The way in
which the prisons of the country are administered,
and the methods by which the criminal classes are
punished and sought to be reformed, will, however,
continue to be a study of interest so long as the
prevention of crime remains a problem of modern
civilisation

Lord Kimberley's Commission recommended the
separation of convicts against whom no previous
conviction is recorded from those who are habitual
offenders, by forming them into a distinct class. This,
if fully carried out, would be reform in the right
direction; but it does not propose to effect such a
complete dissociation of casual from hardened criminals
as will minimise the evils of contamination and weaken
habits and influences that tend to confirm criminal
propensities.   Of the number of convicts undergoing
sentences of penal servitude, not more than five
per cent. have never been in prison before.   In what

manner it was intended by Lord Kimberley's Commission that these five hundred or more "Star" convicts should be formed into a separate class, is not specified in the wording of the recommendation just referred to. Distributed over the various convict prisons, this "Star" class would give about fifty or sixty to each establishment, and unless they are employed apart, as well as located apart, from all the other inmates of each prison, the proposal of the Commission would not be fully carried out, if I rightly apprehend its spirit and object.

To explain the plan of "classification" that is followed in the convict system, as now administered by the Board of Directors, will probably be the best way of drawing attention to the need for a further extension of the reform which was the first of the eleven chief recommendations contained in the Report of the recent Penal Servitude Acts Commission.

All convicts are classed according to the time which they have served out under their respective sentences, and not, as is generally supposed, according to the nature of the crime for which they are convicted, the number of previous convictions, or the duration of sentences. A murderer, a forger, a bigamist, a pickpocket, a burglar, and an issuer of counterfeit coin, if tried and sentenced at the same assize, might all pass together through the five stages of penal servitude—

" probation," " third," " second," " first," and " special "
classes   Assuming that they would be equal in their
obedience to disciplinary regulations, no distinction
whatever would be drawn between them after that
made by the judge in awarding to each different terms
of penal servitude.

Every convict upon entering " probation class " (first
stage after sentence) is given a register number and
" letter " by which he is to be subsequently known—
the letter denoting the year of conviction   Prisoners
sentenced in the year 1874, for instance, have the letter
" A " on the sleeve of the jacket; those in 1875 " B,"
1876 " C," &c.; while those whose trials have occurred
anterior to 1874 are lettered in the reverse order, *e.g*
1873 " Z," 1872 " Y," 1871 " X," &c.   Re-convicted men
wear two or more letters, representing the years in
which their sentences were passed: thus " W " " G "
would mean a first conviction in 1870, and a second
in 1880.

This plan of " classification " is really no classification
at all; or, at least, it bears about the same relation to
what is the obvious meaning of the term, when applied
to a discriminating separation of criminals undergoing
punishment in a convict prison as would the " playing
at soldiers " of a band of children to the regular daily
drill and military efficiency of a company of the line.
Fifty convicts, sentenced, say, last year, will, upon

reaching Dartmoor, Portland, or Portsmouth prisons this year, be located according to their badge-letters, if there should happen to be accommodation in those wards in which prisoners are usually required to pass the second year of their sentence; but while at daily work these fifty new convicts will be distributed among the sixty or eighty labour-gangs into which the inmates of each of these prisons are divided, irrespective of any distinction whatever of crime, duration of sentence, number of previous convictions, or length of sentence worked out

I fail to see any insuperable difficulty, so far as the management of convict prisons is concerned, in the way of extending the classification proposed by Lord Kimberley's Commission to the daily work of convicts, as well as to their location in what are supposed to be separate wards. This would effectively prevent all contact between hardened criminals and those less infected with moral disease

A further separation, regulated on something like a classification of offences, would still more narrow the sphere of contamination, and afford full play to whatever deterrent influence the punishment of penal servitude exercises upon the minds of criminals The force of example is most powerful where there is no moral check upon vicious acts. I have known convicts, not belonging to the thieving classes, become experts

in stealing other prisoners' food from observing the way
in which skilled pickpockets could abstract loaves from
the ward bread-basket, or rifle the cell of a next-door
neighbour. The certainty of punishment deters from
such acts only in proportion to the thief's belief as to
his chances of detection.

I have known some of those perverted beings whose
particular walk in crime will only bear hinting at, to
monopolize the surreptitious conversation of their immediate surroundings in the work-gang by day and of
the ward in which they were located by night. Most
of the cells in the public-works prisons are made of
corrugated iron, and they offer as great a facility for
conversation, when the habits of the warder or the
night-guard in charge are understood, as if no partition
existed between the several sleeping apartments. Men
convicted for unnatural crimes are not very numerous,
it is true, but they should be confined in other than
corrugated iron cells by night, and be employed by
day apart from all other prisoners.

The thieving class—pickpockets, burglars, and
swindlers—should also be located by themselves,
and be debarred from association in daily labour
with those prisoners whose offences do not imply a
confirmed disposition in the individual to prey
upon society. A further division of this, the most
numerous class of criminal, into young and old

offenders, both in respect to location and employment should likewise, for obvious reasons, be effected in each convict prison.

"*Solitary*"—How far the practice of separate confinement should be carried in the punishment and reformation of criminals is a subject upon which more has been written, *pro* and *con*, than on any other phase of penal discipline. The experience of one man can be no test of how solitary confinement affects another; as its influence, for good or evil, must be as various as the temperaments of those subjected to it. It is a subject upon which theory will decide nothing. The only test of its worth, as a reformative agency particularly, is that of experience, and few who have actually acquired this knowledge care to come before the public with their opinions. Those who are next best qualified to speak on the matter are, of course, governors and chaplains of convict prisons, but the opinions of these latter authorities are liable to be influenced by their respective callings —governors will shape their views in accordance with the trouble or facility which separate confinement affords them in maintaining the discipline of their prisons, rather than from its observed effect upon the health or moral character of their prisoners; while prison chaplains, as a rule, value this kind of treatment solely for the opportunities which it offers for imparting religious instruction. I may remark again that the apparently devout "chaplains' and priests' men"—as "religious" prisoners are termed —are *generally* the most hardened criminals, experienced, calculating thieves, and diplomatic swindlers who are too wary to quarrel with the prison rules, and too accustomed to the practice of deception to refrain from imposing, as far as possible, upon priest and minister   Separate confinement has no reformative effect whatever upon this class of criminal, though it exercises a certain, but by no means considerable, punitive one.

My observation of the effect which separate confinement has upon all criminals—accidental, casual, and hardened—leads me to the conclusion, that if the nine months "solitary" in the initial stage of the sentence were changed to six months then and six more at the terminal portion, it would exercise a more deterrent effect than under the existing arrangement.   The one thing most dreaded by the old jail-bird is work requiring bodily exertion.   His fingers become as trained, by practice, in picking oakum when in prison, as in picking pockets or locks when out, and as this is the usual task that has to be performed during solitary confinement, it has no terrors equal to what a barrow or a shovel on public works has for one who hates "hard graft" next to the wages of idleness—bread and water   To be exempted from hard labour is the one object which occupies every mental resource of experienced criminals from the time of sentence until the medical inspection in Millbank or Pentonville shall determine what is to be the class of labour in which the remainder of the sentence is to be passed. It is during "solitary" the plans are laid by which the doctor is to be persuaded that hard labour can only be performed at the risk of certain death; and it is in this stage, likewise, that malingering and kindred practices are most resorted to in hopes of qualifying for an invalid prison. Such of the regular criminal class as are physically able for the performance of hard labour should be transferred as soon as possible after conviction to the public-works prisons, to be put to the work which is really more healthful for them than sedentary labour, but which is, at the same time, more distasteful, and, of all the punishments comprised in penal servitude, is the one best calculated to deter them from incurring the risk of its re-infliction

On the other hand, such convicts as have some record of having worked for a living at one period or another of their lives, dread separate confinement more than the tasks on public works; and as this is the class of prisoners most susceptible of reformation, the kind of treatment to which they are subjected deserves more serious attention than that of the habitual offender. I am no believer in separate confinement as a sovereign remedy for criminal reformation. If it saves some prisoners from contact with more hardened criminals, it is open to the objection of inducing mental and bodily diseases in men who are not hopelessly given over to crime. Under conditions that would lessen the evils just referred to, separate confinement might become a reformative kind of punishment instead of being, what it now is, a portion of the partially deterrent system so elaborately organised by Sir E. F. Du Cane. More rewards, in better food and increased gratuities, for work and exemplary conduct, greater attention on the part of schoolmasters, chaplains, and superior prison officials, with increased privileges in the way of keeping up home influences—such as letters and visits—together with shorter sentences all worked out, would undoubtedly render separate confinement a means of reforming a large number of criminals whose better nature under the kind of penal servitude now inflicted is not only completely ignored, but mechanically reduced to the uniform level of Sir E. F Du Cane's standing army of 10,000 habitual offenders. Such a sweeping reform, however, as one that would substitute shorter terms of punishment passed in improved "solitary" for first convictions, in place of those now inflicted, is more likely to be looked upon as a kind of penal millennium than to be deemed practicable by the military men into whose hands the administration of prisons has completely passed, and by whose expensive management each convict is made to cost the public over thirty pounds a year

Separate confinement at the end of a sentence of penal servitude for "Star" and young convicts would give fuller scope to the deterrent influence of that kind of punishment than it now possesses. It would weaken the effects of the association with other criminals during the working out of the sentence, and enable the reformative agencies of chaplain and schoolmaster to better prepare the prisoner for the world into which he would go direct from their teachings.

Hardened criminals, subject to the classification recommended, with, of course, sufficient healthy food, should be kept at such bodily labour as they are fit to perform from sentence until discharge. Could another penal colony be founded for this type of criminal it would be a blessing to himself and a boon to society to send him there. In England he will but continue to move in a circle of crime and imprisonment. Change of surroundings develops change of disposition in individuals. Admitting the evils that were associated with the penal settlement in Australia, it cannot be denied but that it rendered material service alike to the colonists and to the transported convicts, many of whom were reclaimed under the new conditions of existence. I have spoken on this subject of a revival of transportation with large numbers of men who are put down as confirmed criminals, but whom I believe to be only conditionally so, and they have invariably declared they would stand a chance of getting along in life, independently of crime, if removed from the haunts and influences which fix their careers at home, and from the society that repels them. Chance for moral retrievement in England there is none. The stigma of penal servitude is not more lasting than is the professional prejudice of the detective police against "a convict at large," or one who is known to these emissaries of the law to have once been convicted of theft. Philanthropic police administrators lead the public to believe in the existence of a London police that neither annoys discharged convicts nor prevents them from gaining an honest livelihood. I am not going to call into question the sincerity of their motives; but if these officials could personally supervise the action of each detective policeman, or indoctrinate their subordinates generally with their own humane opinions, they would only then be in a position to give such an assurance to the public As well suppose a trained dog capable of refraining from pursuing game as expect men who obtain their living by tracking, and earn promotion by efficiency

in detecting, criminals, to look with any feeling of
compassion upon "a known thief" after his liberation
from prison. To watch discharged convicts is the sole
duty of select detective officers, and this surveillance
alone, if its performance could be freed from the
prejudice of the force against those whom they believe belong to the confirmed criminal class, would
necessitate the disclosure of the antecedents of an
ex-convict to whoever might be induced, through
ignorance of the same, to give him employment of
any trust   I do not say that the detective police, as
a body, systematically prevent discharged prisoners
from gaining an honest livelihood; but I assert that
it is absurd to suppose that they are more considerate
of the interests of the man whom they are trained to
look upon as a confirmed criminal than of those of
an employer of labour, who, they naturally enough
believe, runs the risk of being victimised unless warned
of the record of the ex-jail-bird who may have succeeded in entering his employment. The re-conviction
of such a large number of criminals proves either
their unwillingness or their inability to earn an
honest living, and sound sense demands the creation
of some scheme whereby their course of life, made up
of theft and punishment in England, should be diverted
into a sphere of existence less harmful to society and
themselves. A penal colony appears to me the only

remedy for confirmed criminals that will combine
a regard for public interests with the dictates of
common humanity

Re-Convicted Criminals—It is not just to rank all
those as habitually criminal who have two sentences of
penal servitude recorded against them. A first conviction may have been brought about through acts
prompted by motives that are not criminal, such as the
pressure of want, or other similar extenuating incentives to a transgression of the law; while the fallibility
of circumstantial and the unconscious bias of interested
evidence may reasonably be supposed to be responsible
for a large percentage of the numerous convictions that
are obtained on the testimony of members of a police
organisation in which there is, naturally enough, en-
gendered a belief in the guilt of every one arrested who
cannot prove him or her self perfectly innocent of a
charge resting upon suspicion

Allowing for the existence of a large number of
prisoners who asseverate their innocence of the crimes of
which they have been clearly proved to be guilty, there
must, nevertheless, be cases in which the machinery of
the law, sharing the imperfections of human nature,
will have been the only offender against justice   One
of many such instances that came under my notice
while confined in Dartmoor convict prison, will
illustrate the terrible wrong which has been not

unfrequently inflicted upon men who have once fallen beneath the ban of the law and the subsequent surveillance of the police

Two convicts, named O'Brien and Bentley, were occasional work-companions of mine, during my stay in that prison, the one having been condemned to fourteen and the other to twenty years' penal servitude, and Bentley being a "second-timer" or re-convicted prisoner. A very strong antipathy that manifested itself between them led me to inquire into its origin, whereupon I discovered that Bentley had been convicted for a burglary of a most daring character that had been committed in London by O'Brien, previous to and independent of the crime for which the latter had been sentenced to fourteen years. The police had failed to trace the deed to the actual perpetrator. Unfortunately for Bentley he was found loitering near the scene of the transaction, and, having a previous conviction against him, he was awarded twenty years' penal servitude—twelve of which he had already served when the foregoing facts were elicited by me, not from Bentley alone, but from O'Brien, the actual author of the crime, and from other prisoners also, who were fully conversant with the whole story of the burglary

It is among "third-" and "fourth-timers," having an additional record of imprisonments in county jails, that the really hardened and irreclaimable type of thief and accomplished swindler is to be found—men whom nothing but the knowledge that they are known to and constantly dogged by the agents of the law will deter from attempting, at all times the gratification of their desire for whatever in the possession of others may chance to excite it.

Non-Discriminating Discipline.—The discipline of convict prisons has been regulated by what is necessary to maintain the most insubordinate prisoner in constant subjection, and not by a standard of what is required to keep in order, and measure out a just and reasonable daily punishment to, the average type of fairly-conducted prisoners. This is a principle that may have suggested to those who legislate for Ireland the idea of imposing a penalty by way of tax upon any district in which an individual has committed some outrage. The result must necessarily be the same in each case. A penalty imposed upon a community for acts for which they are not collectively responsible is certain to breed more of discontent towards the power that inflicts it than resentment against the person alone morally and justly blamable in the transaction A prisoner in Dartmoor was one day discovered with a piece of iron concealed beneath his vest, whereupon an order was immediately put in force compelling *all* prisoners to bare their chests to the shirt, in future, on each of the four occasions, daily, when searching on parade took place. When the dampness of the climate of Dartmoor is borne in mind—the rainfall averaging more than 100 inches in the year—it can easily be seen how much additional punishment was thus unmeritedly inflicted upon a thousand convicts for an act committed by one; and how coughs and colds would necessarily be multiplied through this needless additional stripping in the open air.

Again, evidence is given before the Royal Commission on the working of the Penal Servitude Acts that the conversation of a certain class of criminal is corrupting to other prisoners, and forthwith we have *all* conversation prohibited to *all* convicts, from the day of their sentence to that of liberation; though upon what authority, beyond that of Sir E. F. Du Cane, this most drastic regulation has been put in force is not easy to determine, as it is not included in the recommendations contained in the Report of Lord Kimberley and his colleagues, nor authorised, so far as I am aware, by any specific parliamentary enactment.

In this prison of Portland, containing an average of sixteen hundred convicts, penal discipline is probably more rigidly carried out than in any other similar establishment in the world. Yet, notwithstanding the daily ordeal of this punishment—its merciless disregard of human passion and feeling, its exaction of implicit obedience to humiliating, minute, and ceaseless regulations which are calculated to keep in sleepless activity every incentive to rebellion of which the human mind is capable under the keenest provocation that could possibly be devised, short of systematic torture—there are *eight hundred criminals against whom there is not a single scratch of a pen* (to use the language of Governor Clifton) *from year to year!* Four hundred more are put down as "good-conducted prisoners," whose casual breaches of the rules are of a trivial character, while an additional two hundred are classed as "fairly conducted" men, who are seldom reported for any act of insubordination requiring the intervention of the visiting director. If such a marvellous command of temper and exercise of obedience as are thus displayed by men whose misfortunes in life are attributable to want of moral self-control in society, could be equalled by righteous men in religious adversity, Job would be surpassed as an exemplar of patience, and half the saints would, in comparison, be deemed unworthy of the calendar. Still, these men, so tried and so exemplary, are subjected to the same discipline, undergo the same degree of labour-punishment daily, and are placed in almost every respect on an exact par with the remaining two hundred more or less reckless prisoners, whose insubordinate dispositions determine the daily regulations and penalties to which all convicts are subjected.

Sentences.—When we think of the enormous wealth that is constantly displayed in London and other large cities to the curious gaze of hundreds of thousands of destitute men, women, and children—creatures who are strangers to the ordinary comforts of life, and for whom the sight of surrounding luxuries must be a kindred torture to that of Tantalus—it is surprising that fifty times more theft is not attempted, and that the criminal class is not far more numerous in Great Britain than we find it to be. It is in connection with these temptations that are exhibited to indigence and vice, often so carelessly, and, as a rule, so needlessly, by the possessors of wealth, that I would direct attention to the unreasonable, if not vindictive, severity of the law in dealing with a class of human beings for whose Ishmaelite propensities society itself is, in the main, responsible. Doubtless human nature has a conception of some moral obligation, or human ideas of right and wrong would not have formed a basis for codes of equity and morals in society. But such a conception, if not nursed and cultivated in the individual by external influences, will no more fructify into correct notions of duty to man and society than would the most fruitful

soil spontaneously offer us the necessaries of life without the hand of labour or the skill of the husbandman
supplying the media by which Nature is delivered of
her gifts to mankind   Given, therefore, a percentage
of the population of Great Britain upon whom poverty
and ignorance are allowed to exercise their demoralising
influence, and upon whose perverted lives the accessory
evils of intemperance and the solicitations of ostentatious
wealth are permitted to have full play, how can the
society that is responsible for such a state of things
sanction the   sentences   that   are   now   passed   upon
criminals who have been thus nurtured by its own
neglect, and for crimes which are mainly the outcome
of its own defective police organisation ?

If it is not denied that even a criminal has a right to
know, before transgressing the law, what is to be the
penalty he is to incur if found guilty of crime, is it not
equally just to say that those who have received no
moral training—the waifs and strays of populous cities,
from whom the criminal class is chiefly recruited—are
not cognisant of the moral obliquity of the acts for
which they receive such enormously disproportionate sentences ?   Are not the incentives to crime more powerful
and numerous than the preventives, say, ꞏ London,
Glasgow, Liverpool, Manchester, and Birmingham—
ities that contribute more than fifty per cent. to the

criminal population of Great Britain? Yet those who are permitted to graduate in criminal pursuits under the tuition of the low drinkhouse and the brothel, and to be subject to the demoralisation of crowded and ill-ventilated dwellings in the slums of cities and towns, are dealt with by the administrators of the law as if they were offending against a society that had done its utmost to remove the nurseries of social disease which breed the convict population of Portland and its kindred establishments. Attention has often been called to the anomalous custom of apportioning the duration of sentences to criminals, by which periods of five, seven, ten, fifteen, twenty years and life are awarded, while penalties comprising intermediate terms are scarcely ever inflicted ; though it would be ridiculous to suppose that intermediate terms would not afford adequate punishment. If regard for the prison accommodation of a growing criminal class, and for the expenditure which their costly system of punishment entails upon the public, induces public writers to ventilate in the press the question of shorter sentences, it may be permissible to add to such arguments the higher ones of simple justice and equity, which are enforced by the above considerations.

The recent Commission for inquiring into the working of the Penal Servitude Acts has recommended the

repeal of that provision in the Penal Servitude Act of
1864 by which, in case where any person is convicted
of any offence punishable with penal servitude after
having been previously convicted of felony, the least
sentence of penal servitude that can be awarded is a
period of seven years. This recommendation is both
just and humane. Why, then, can there not be discovered a virtue of punishment in terms of four, six,
eight, nine, eleven, twelve, sixteen and eighteen years
respectively, as well as in "the favourite periods" of
five, seven, ten, fifteen and twenty?   It is absurdly
unjust to proceed upon the theory that because ten
years is deemed by a judge to be insufficient punishment for an offence which does not merit fourteen, there
is therefore no intermediate figure that could satisfy
the ends of justice.

Quality of Punishment.—It could be nowise deroga-
tory to the functions of those whose occupation it is to
pass sentence upon criminals to pay periodical visits to
the various convict establishments, in order to obtain a
fuller insight into what penal discipline really is, and
what is the true nature of the punishment that is
awarded in a sentence of five, ten, or fifteen years of
convict slavery. Such knowledge would be easily purchased if it disclosed to judicial minds the fact that the
quality of the punishment to which convicts are sub-

jected is calculated to engender among criminals the feeling that the law has been vindictive where it should only have been just; and that there is inflicted in a five-years' sentence of such a system of purgatorial expiation, as that now perfected by Sir E. F. Du Cane, a penalty far more severe than what is believed by the general public to be comprised in penal servitude.

When prison officials are seen coming forward to advocate—as they occasionally do in the magazines—a non-vindictive policy towards the criminal classes, the public mind is edified by the spectacle of philanthropy being associated with the control of the prisons of the country and the police of London; and he must indeed be an ungrateful tax-payer who will begrudge whatever annual sum is asked from Parliament to maintain in efficiency the systems so administered If these public servants could infuse their own fairness into every member of the subdivided machinery of their centralised departments, there would no longer be any fear of an unwarranted exercise of deputed authority on the part of subordinates. It must not, however, be overlooked in an estimate of this kind, that it is natural in all responsible officials to persuade themselves, and the public if possible, that a degree of perfection has been reached in their special posts of trust not previously attained therein. The reputation for efficiency of a prominent public officer is too frequently accepted as a guarantee for that of his department Confidence in the head suggests belief in the soundness of the whole of the machinery supposed to be under his immediate hand. In the administration of centralised civic authority this is anything but a safe guide to a correct knowledge as to the just and impartial exercise of its duties. Where there is but indirect control in the performance of such duties as those of a prison warder, there cannot be direct supervision, and deputed prison authority is liable to abuse in exact proportion to the relative legal status of the officer and the convict What, for instance, does the chairman of directors know of the full nature of convict Smith's punishment under the rule of assistant-warder Jones, in the quarries outside our cell or on the bogs of Dartmoor ? If Smith reports Jones's petty tyranny to the governor, all that Jones has to do, to evade whatever consequences such treatment might incur, is to deny the truth of the charge, and, according to the evidence of prison governors tendered to Lord Kimberley's Commission, the officer's denial would dispose of the matter. But Smith's injury would not end here, if he were foolish enough to report his officer, even under provocation. The giving of marks to convicts, by which remission of sentence is alone earned, is the duty of warders and assistant-warders, and the stoppage of even two marks for one day, out of a possible daily earning of eight, might entail upon Smith a prolongation of penal servitude for one week.

To inquire into a circumstance of this kind (with hundreds of which I have been familiar during my imprisonment in Dartmoor), Sir E. F. Du Cane would have to receive his information through the various grades of authority interposing between himself and convict Smith; and yet with this disadvantage, as to a correct knowledge of the real character of the punishment of penal servitude, as carried out by practically irresponsible subordinates, Sir E. F. Du Cane is expected to say whether such a penalty, so inflicted, is calculated to reform or harden the criminal

Penal servitude has become so elaborated that it is now a huge punishing machine, destitute, through centralised control and responsibility, of discrimination, feeling, or sensitiveness; and its non-success as a deterrent from crime, and complete failure in reformative effect upon criminal character, are owing to its obvious essential tendency to deal with erring human beings—who are still men despite their crimes—in a manner which mechanically reduces them to a uniform level of disciplined brutes.

There is scarcely a crime possible for man to be guilty of, short of murder, which should not, in strict justice, be expiated by seven years' infliction of a punishment that has been brought to such a nicet of calculation that there is the closest possible surveillance of every one undergoing it night and day, together with an unceasing conflict between every feeling in the prisoner that is superior to a mere condition of animal existence and the everlasting compulsion to refrain from almost all that it is natural for man to do, and to do what it is to the last degree repugnant for any rational being to consent to perform. Yet wretches who have had a London gutter or a workhouse for their only moral training-school, and who have been subsequently nurtured in crime by society's other licensed agencies of moral corruption, receive ten, fifteen, and sometimes twenty years for thefts and crimes which should, in justice, be expiated by a twelve months' duration of such punishment It is these horribly unjust penalties that beget many of the desperadoes of Portland, Chatham, and Dartmoor, the murderers of warders, the malingerers, and the partial maniacs, and which implant in the minds of convicts that ferocious animosity against law and society which turns so many of them into reckless social savages A chastisement that would punish criminals without keeping in perpetual motion all that is vicious and resentful in human nature, and, while inflicting a merited penalty for proven guilt, should teach a better lesson to erring humanity than despair and revenge, would surely serve the ends of law and justice without impairing the systems of detection and punishment by which society is protected from its enemies

END OF VOL. I

LONDON
R CLAY, SONS, AND TAYLOR
BREAD STREET HILL

CPSIA information can be obtained at www.ICGtesting.com
Printed in the USA
LVOW061924060313

323028LV00007B/274/P